EUSAPIA PALADINO

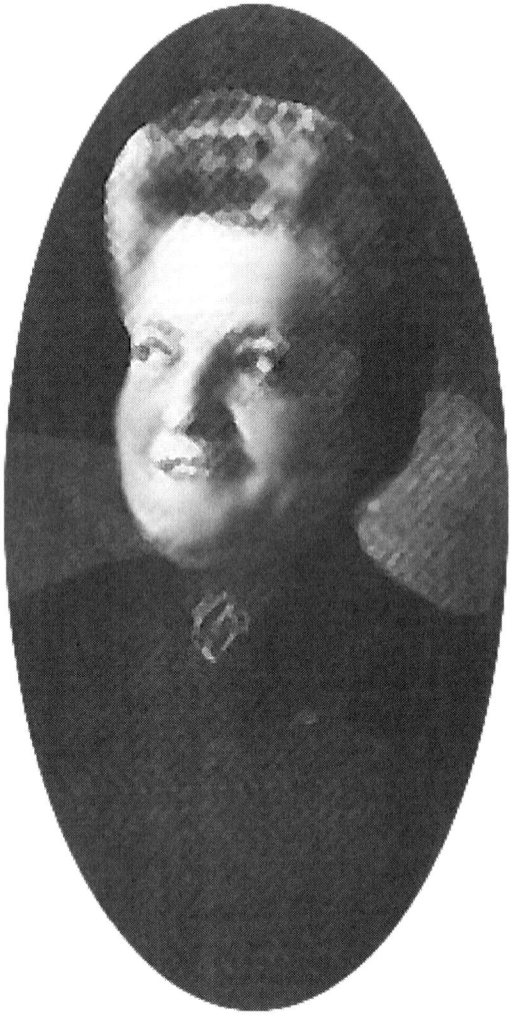

Eusapia Paladino
Materialisations and Intellergetic Phenomena
in Physical Mediumship

compiled and edited
by
Scott Dickerson

Lost Foundations of Parapsychology and
Psychical Research

eyewitness accounts
method and credibility
experimental analysis
criticism

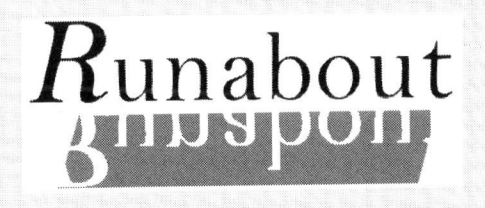

Runabout

LOST FOUNDATIONS OF PARAPSYCHOLOGY AND
PSYCHICAL RESEARCH

Eusapia Paladino
MATERIALISATIONS AND INTELLERGETIC PHENOMENA
IN PHYSICAL MEDIUMSHIP

COPYRIGHT © 2016
SCOTT DICKERSON

ALL RIGHTS RESERVED

PRINTED IN THE UNITED STATES OF AMERICA

Contents

INTRODUCTION: The Spiritistic and 11
Spiritualistic Explanation of
Mediumistic Phenomena
[*from* THE ANNALS OF PSYCHICAL SCIENCE,
Vol. VI, July-December 1907]

A Contribution to the Study 41
of Materialisations
[*from* THE ANNALS OF PSYCHICAL SCIENCE,
Vol. VI, July-December 1907]

ON THE THRESHOLD OF 139
THE UNSEEN:
Eusapia Paladino
[*published* KEEGAN PAUL 1917
Second Edition (revised)]

PSYCHICAL AND SUPERNORMAL 147
PHENOMENA:
Experiments Made With
Eusapia Paladino at Genoa
by Professor Morselli
[*published* WILLIAM RIDER & SON, LTD 1916]

The Naples Sittings of 1908 170
[*from* THE REPORT PRESENTED TO THE SOCIETY FOR PSYCHICAL RESEARCH 1908]

MODERN SPIRITUALISM, ... 191
A HISTORY AND CRITICISM:
Eusapia Paladino
[*published* Methuen & Company
1902]

AFTER DEATH—WHAT? 201
Experiments With Eusapia
[*first published* 1909]

Biographical Sketch of.................................. 284
Eusapia Paladino
[*from* THE ANNALS OF PSYCHICAL SCIENCE,
Vol. VI, July-December 1907]

The American Seances of 1908 253
[*from* THE NEW YORK WORLD,
THE NEW YORK TIMES, AND
THE NEW YORK WORLD 1909]

EUSAPIA PALADINO

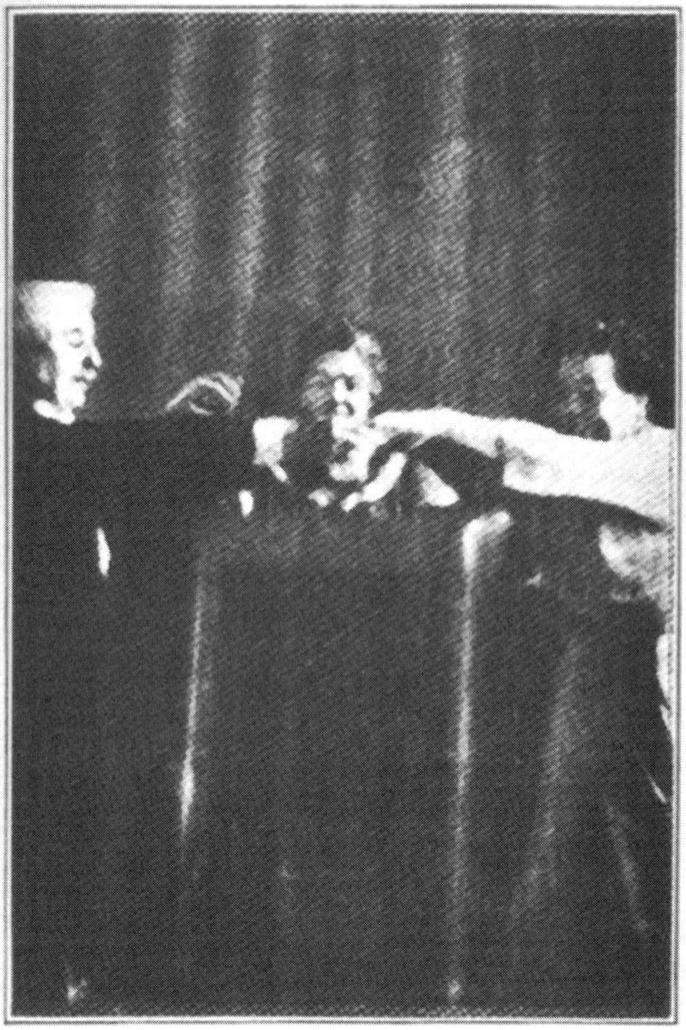

INTRODUCTION:
The Spiritistic and Spiritualistic Explanation of Mediumistic Phenomena

By CÆSAR DE VESME
(ANNALS, AUG 1907)

1. PREFACE

THE IMMENSE impression produced in Italy by the reports of the séances which several Italian *savants* have held with Eusapia Paladino, offers fresh confirmation of the truth, upon which I have continually insisted in this journal, namely, that it is only experiments made by savants which have the power of moving public opinion and influencing it in favour of the reality of these metapsychical facts. Following the celebrated declarations made by Professors Lombroso, Morselli, Foà, the assistants of Prof. Mosso, and numerous other doctors, we have the account of some recent experiments conducted by a group of Professors in the University of Naples, which experiments have given the best results ; there is also the levitation of the body of the medium observed by Profs. Murani and Patrizi with the medium Zuccarini. And the movement progresses with increasing rapidity, fresh names of *savants* being constantly added to those of Profs. Lombroso, Schiaparelli, Luciani, De Amicis, Bianchi, Queirolo, Gigli, Vizioli, Tamburini,

Tassi, Ascensi, Porro, Limoncelli, Virgilio, Giardina, Ottolenghi, etc.—all being Professors in the Universities of Italy, for the most part also psychiatrists and physiologists, who had already recognised and testified to the supernormal phenomena produced by Eusapia.

It is difficult to realise the effect which has been produced on all classes of society in Italy by these conversions of men of science. The principal journals in Northern Italy have openly declared their intention of freely opening their columns to publications bearing reference to mediumism, of which they recognise the immense scientific and social importance. A Milanese doctor, passing through Turin, wrote to me lately:

> I knew of the impression that had been produced in Milan by the recent declarations of *savants*, and by the courageous campaign undertaken by various organs of the Press. But public opinions has not less largely changed in Turin, especially since Prof. Foà's lecture in the Carignan Theatre. A few weeks ago it was impossible to say two words about spiritistic phenomena without being answered by a shrug of the shoulders ; now, however, these same facts no longer arouse hostility, but only a slight doubt blended with curiosity and sympathy. We may argue from his how easily the ideas of the public on this question might be changed from top to bottom, if only the spiritists, instead of contenting themselves with the communications which purport to come from the spirits of Campanella and Mazzini, and such like, had the acuteness to attract *savants* to their circles.

I am entirely of the same opinion. It would be only a matter of three or four years for metapsychical phenomena to pass from the domain of the pre-scientific to the domain of the scientific, if only there could be formed, in some large centre, a group of a few whole-hearted, devoted men of *modern and practical ideas*, possessing, in marked degree, the "fighting spirit," never likely to lose themselves in the fog of scientific abstractions, but bringing into this struggle of ideas the habitual systems of all great humanitarian struggles, whether social or political.

But it is most important to point out that the revival of interest in these questions, which has been displayed by the public in Italy, would not have been produced so easily, if the scientific men who have just proclaimed the objective authenticity of these mediumistic phenomena had not been careful to add that the recognition of the *facts* does not by any means imply the acceptance of the spiritistic hypothesis. For, in truth, the greatest obstacle which the metapsychical propaganda encounters has been raised by the spiritists themselves. They have worked so well and in such a way during the last thirty years that many people who approach the consideration of mediumistic phenomena imagine that they cannot admit these without at the same time accepting as authentic all the "messages from beyond the grave," signed by more or less illustrious names, and the whole philosophy of (Andrew) Jackson Davis or Allan Kardec with the "seven spheres," "reincarnation" and all the rest. A much larger number suppose that they will be bound necessarily to admit that the "spirits" that manifest are the souls of the deceased, and can be nothing else. A great number also think that the acceptance of the objective character of the phenomena cannot, at least, be disconnected from belief in "spirits" of some sort. Let us once get rid of these mistaken notions, and let us make it clear that it is possible to accept the *facts*, without giving adherence to such or such a theory, and we shall, at the same time remove the dislike which mediumistic phenomena inspire alike in the minds of reasoners, of the followers of various religions or philosophies, and of materialists, etc.

From the point of view of advisability, therefore, we can congratulate ourselves on the methods followed by the Italian *savants* of whom we have spoken. It is for these reasons that I have been glad to reproduce their words in the ANNALS, and thus to make them known more particularly to the scientific and medical men who are so numerous among the readers of our two editions. We say this, without any intention, of course, of accusing the *savants* in question of *opportunism* ; the sincerity of their opinions cannot give occasion to a shadow of doubt. But can we say the same from the point of view of truth and logic? Should we, in order not to renounce a dangerous method of tactics, countenance that which we believe to be, or may become, error, and suffer the criticism of a number of scientific men to stray into false paths into which they will not fail to draw a numerous following of imitators? I think that a calm and courteous consideration of this point of view will not be inappropriate at the present moment, and will prevent many future contests when misunderstanding may have taken such deep root as not to be easily eradicated.

2. A PRIORISM IN SCIENTIFIC LANGUAGE

An understanding is now rendered easier by the fact that there is no question of difference as to *principle*, but merely as to the way in which the principle should be applied. Ever since Professor Sidgwick, of the University of Cambridge, accepted the position of first President of the Society for Psychical Research, London, and gave a strictly positive direction to the study of supernormal psychic phenomena, everyone of a scientific bent who has considered these questions, has recognised the primary importance of examining the facts from the objective point of view, and of carrying this objectivity into the terms employes. No thoughtful, serious spiritualist even would now venture to say, for example, that "a *spirit* had appeared," that "a medium had written under the influence of a such or such a deceased person," etc. They know that it is better to say "that a *human form*," or at least, in certain eases, "that a *phantom* appeared," that a medium wrote under the influence *of an intelligence* "*purporting*" to be a particular deceased person, etc. They have gone further: they have learnt not to say, for example, that "a certain person *appeared* to another at the moment of death," but that they should simply say: "the apparition coincided with the moment of the death of the person whose features it reproduced." And so forth. It is recognised that we cannot speak otherwise without pre-judging in some degree the *interpretation* of the fact, an interpretation which should be reserved, and kept distinct from, the *fact* itself, since the latter may constitute an *objective* reality, whilst the *interpretation* can only be *subjective*. For simplicity's sake, we sometimes have recourse to the expedient of placing the words "spirit," "spiritistic" phenomena, etc., between inverted commas ; otherwise we could not free ourselves from the embarrassments of language in certain lengthy and intricate arguments. Professor Morselli has made considerable use of this expedient in his article ; a spiritist who translated the article for a Parisian journal thought he was at liberty to overlook these troublesome little commas, the use of which he probably did not perceive, and hence a character was given to the article for which the author can hardly be grateful! In some cases, we are all apt to be neglectful of this precision, this propriety of scientific language. But we must not excuse ourselves ; that would be unwise ; let us confess that we are not then writing at our best ; at the most, the only excuse we can make in our defence is, that "*Quandoque bonus dormitat Homerus.*"

Let us, however, force ourselves to keep awake. But it is a very different thing when a man of Science deliberately uses this *subjective* form of language with the obvious assumption that he is, on the contrary, using scientific and objective terms. That is an error whteh I think it is my duty to denounce.

Let us take, for instance, the following phrases from the reports of Drs. Herlitzka, Ch. Foà, and Aggazzotti, the assistants of Prof. Mosso:

> "Dr. Herlitzka asked for permission to seize the lid ; *the medium consented through the table, which rapped three times.*" ... "Then seven raps informed us that the *medium wished to terminate the séance...*"

We might multiply examples. It is obvious that this language is quite as *a prioristic* in character as that used by the more numerous, but less enlightened, section of spiritists. It is perhaps even more so, because spiritists might allege that they use the term *spirit* to simplify language, instead of saying "the Intelligence *which purports to be a spirit*" ; but in the terms used by Prof. Mosso's assistants, the intention of bending the facts to fit the interpretation which they choose to put upon them, is indisputable. They might have said in quite objective terms "The intelligence which regulated the movements of the table rapped three times," or quite simply "the table gave three raps, which signified yes." They were careful not to do so ; they wished to indicate their scientific way of regarding the phenomena, and they have in reality fallen into the same error as that of less enlightened spiritists, although in the reverse direction. Certainly they took care to inform us in another place that they came to the conclusion that all the phenomena they had observed were direct manifestations of the conscious or unconscious will of the medium ; that all phenomena were announced beforehand by the medium, or suggested by those present ; that they were all accompanied by muscular contractions on the part of the medium. But we know also that other critics of much worth have formed a contrary opinion—that it is quite incorrect that "all the phenomena are announced beforehand by the medium or suggested by those present," —but that even if this were so, it would prove nothing, since the medium, when announcing the phenomena, often speaks under the influence of a personality purporting to be a "spirit," the quality of which assertion we cannot *a priori* contest ; — that out of the phenomena suggested by the medium, some are produced and some are not produced, and others again are produced in a very different manner from that desired (as occurred, for instance, with the the instruments prepared by Prof. Mosso's assistants), and this quite permits us to suppose the intervention of an independent intelligence which accepts, refuses, or modifies the proposals of those present ; —finally, "the muscular contractions of the medium which accompany the phenomena" prove absolutely nothing, because they would exist even if the phenomena were directed by a "spirit," since in any case, according to the spiritistic hypothesis, the medium contributes to the production of the phenomena, by her nervous, fluidic, and other forces. Whether entities from the Beyond do or do not intervene in mediumistic phenomena, we cannot and we ought not to affirm *a priori*. When we have to state that the table has rapped three times, it is quite as much *a prioristic* and hence unscientific, to say that the medium has thus made known her will as to say that a spirit has so done—this not being the statement of a *fact* but of an *of opinion*.

3. A Priorism in Ideas

It will not, however be imagined that it is merely a question of form, however important that may be, which is the subject of the present article. I have no doubt, moreover, that the men who are the collaborators of Professor A. Mosso in his laboratory will entirely agree with me in recognising this scientific rule which, doubtless, they infringed merely by inadvertence. If I have pointed out this error in the form of reporting a séance, it is because it contributes largely to show up a tendency of mind which we encounter not only in the three doctors in question, but also in Prof. Morselli and in Prof. Pio Foà, in their dissertations which we published in our issues for May and June. This tendency originates in a preconceived idea which is very widespread at the present time, as much in scientific circles as among the masses and which may be thus defined: *It is a scientific axiom that the purely materialistic hypothesis concerning the nature of man is more scientific than the dual or spiritualistic hypothesis.*

It is against this *a priori* theory, which nothing justifies, that we are bound to protest if we wish to place the subject on a true scientific basis.

In order to form a just estimate of this subject, we must try to view it from one aspect only (which no doubt is rather difficult), that of the enormous ignorance of modern science concerning the psychic nature of man. Only a year ago, Prof. A. Binet, who is one of the best authorities in pure, official psychology, gave in his *Année Psychologique* a *résumé* of the debates on the *monistic* or *dual* nature of the human being, somewhat to this effect, that when we balance the arguments used to support either of these two hypotheses against the other, we shall find perhaps that they are of about equal weight. Sir Oliver Lodge, in his recent work, *Life and Matter*, after having shown the unfoundedness of the theories on which Ernest Hæckel bases his materialist Bible, *The Riddle of the Universe*, writes:

> "He is, as it were, a surviving voice from the middle of the Nineteenth Century; he represents, in clear and eloquent fashion, opinions which then were prevalent among many leaders of thought—opinions which they themselves in many cases, and their successors still more, lived to outgrow; so that by this time Professor Hæckel's voice is as the voice of one crying in the wilderness—not as the pioneer of vanguard of an advancing army, but as the despairing shout of a standard-bearer, still bold and unflinching, but abandoned by the retreating ranks of his comrades, as they march to new orders in a fresh and more idealistic direction."

Prof. William James, in a recent series of lectures, showed that the thesis of certain physiologists, according to which thought is a "function of the brain," "whilst probably correct, may simply signify that the brain has not a *productive* function, but solely a *permissive* and *transmissive* function." Let us pass by all that part of *The Riddle of The Universe* which relates to the scientific errors which we meet with in the theology of the various religions; these need not detain us. At a certain point, however, Hæckel finds himself face to face with the question of the phenomena termed "Spiritistic," and this is how he treats it:

> "Where the alleged marvels of spiritism have been thoroughly investigated, they have been traced to a more or less clever deception; the mediums, generally of the weaker sex, have been found to be either smart swindlers or nervous persons of abnormal irritability."

One more remark, and that is all. If Profs. Morselli, Foà, etc., will give a glance at the work: "*The Origin of Psychic Phenomena*," by one of their colleagues in the University of Rome, Hæckel's lieutenant, Prof. Sergi, what will they find concerning supernormal psychic facts in this book on psychic phenomena? Quite simply, nothing at all. Not because Prof. Sergi has never heard of them, far from it, but he thinks it useless to pay any attention to them, since, in his opinion, they do not exist. He has, moreover, clearly explained his opinion on the subject in a pamphlet on *Spiritism* which he has published. It is needless to multiply quotations to prove the ingenuity with which the leaders of materialist thought have rid themselves of the difficulty which metapsychical phenomena might cause them.

Unfortunately for them, Profs. Morselli, Foà, etc., had the opportunity of being present at some mediumistic séances, and they now *know* that the phenomena called "spiritistic" exist. They know it like all other experimenters who have sought and found the opportunity of being present at a few good séances with a good medium.

There are then psychologists, physiologists, etc., who pretend to know the essence of human matter to such an extent as to be able to resolve the "riddle of the Universe," or to discover the origin of psychic phenomena in such wise that they can draw the deduction that no manifestation from the Beyond is revealed to humanity, and yet who ignore psychical and physiological phenomena of such enormous importance that it seems as if they would upset all the ideas of modern science concerning the human *psyche*. It has come to this, that simpleminded spiritists, gifted with common sense, who have empirically recognised the existence of these supernormal facts, are nearer to the truth than the revered scientific men who still deny them, just as all those who believed in "Animal Magnetism," during the first half of last century, were nearer to the truth than the *savants* who contested the phenomena of magnetism—and that even if it should ultimately be proved that all hypnotic phenomena are produced by suggestion without the intervention of any magnetic fluid.

In one of his last addresses to the Society for Psychical Research (London), Frederick Myers brought forward a fact which helps to explain this situation. Certain Greek writers have told us that, in the temple of Ephesus, there was carefully preserved a stone which Jupiter in his wrath had thrown down from heaven on to the earth. Astronomers and meteorologists necessarily supposed this tradition to be merely a fable, until about a hundred years ago. Nowadays we perfectly understand that this stone was an aerolite. Superstitious antiquity in its belief therefore approached the real truth far more nearly than the Science which, only a century ago, denied the fall of meteorites. But now it is no longer a question merely of magnetism or of the fall of a few stones upon our globe ; the question relates to phenomena of such extraordinary importance that Prof. Foà in his address (ANNALS, page 438), expressed his opinion that the study of mediums possesses an interest "which is infinitely superior" to the study of hypnotic or neuropathic subjects or of insanity or criminality. What will remain, in fact, of the classical idea which modern psychologists entertain concerning the human *psyche* if we face the psychical phenomena called "supernormal?" Perhaps only a tenth part. And I am going to prove it.

4. Concerning the Opinion that Phenomena Should be Explicable by One and the Same Master Hypothesis

First of all, in order to prepare the ground we should be clear about one point of the question. It is constantly being repeated that the theory which is able to explain *all* metapsychical phenomena has not yet been discovered ; Prof. Morselli lays great emphasis on this point. When passing in review the various hypotheses which have been put forward in order to account for mediumistic phenomena, he says, with reference, for instance, to the telepathic hypothesis:

"In my opinion, telepathy might explain the

clairvoyance displayed in various 'spirit messages' and perhaps also 'the identification of Spirits,' ... but not physical action at a distance, raps, materialisations, etc." (ANNALS, June, 1907, p. 413.)

He therefore seeks elsewhere the explanation which should act as a key to the comprehension of all mediumistic phenomena. After this fashion, when we are considering the hypotheses which will explain physical phenomena such as raps, materialisations etc., we must reject them because they do not serve to explain mental phenomena such as "spirit messages," telepathy, etc. Now, we must insist on this point: that we shall never find the one master hypothesis which will furnish us with the key to *all* metapsychical phenomena, simply because it is practically certain that these phenomena possess different origins. But what does that signify? Astronomers do not reject the hypothesis of the rotation or of the revolution of the Earth merely because neither of the hypotheses alone is sufficient to explain both the succession of days and nights, and the succession of the seasons. On the contrary, they have accepted both. They complete one another. We should treat metapsychical phenomena similarly, abandoning the vain attempt to find the master-key, the single interpretation which will apply to them all.

5. SHOWING HOW MEDIUMISTIC PHENOMENA GRADUALLY TEND TO SUGGEST THE EXISTENCE OF "SPIRITS" AND FLUIDIC BODIES

But if the hypotheses which must serve to explain metapsychical phenomena are almost certainly manifold, it is not less true that they are connected in such a way that their combination forms one great synthetised hypothesis. Myers has embodied this synthesis in an admirable fashion, in his *Human Personality*, which Sir Oliver Lodge has declared may become the *Novum Organum* of the psychological science of the future, if the reality of the various kinds of metapsychical phenomena of which Myers affirms the existence becomes recognised. Is their reality now duly proved ? Almost all the savants who have studied these questions think not, and, for my part, this is also my humble opinion. But if the ocean of the human *psyche* has not yet been sounded to its depths, we may say that the portion nearest to the shore—the shallowest portion—has begun to be thus sounded. And here is what investigators have discovered.

First with regard to the mind,—if indeed there is any exact and real distinction between mind and matter—, they have proved the existence of a latent stratum of the human mind, which has been termed the "subliminal consciousness," and which is not identical with that which classical psychology denotes as the "subconscious," the latter only registering notions perceived in a "normal" fashion and only possessing "normal" faculties. (By this word *normal*, I intend here to denote the modes of perception recognised to-day by official science.) Those faculties which, as we have just said, belong to the latent condition of our consciousness, rise to the surface on occasions, particularly in the case of certain individuals, in a rudimentary, fugitive and incomplete way. The subliminal consciousness has been represented by an apt illustration, as the submerged portion of a ship, hiding in its hold the most precious cargo, the portion which emerges from the water representing the supraliminal consciousness. The portions of the hold which are near the surface of the water are visible here and there, from time to time, according to the motion made by the waves. This subliminal consciousness, still but little known has its "supernormal" and mysterious faculties, to which have been empirically given the names of telepathy (if this phenomenon is, indeed, purely psychological in character as Myers believed), clairvoyance, psychometry, telæsthesia, premonition, etc. These phenomena are proved by numerous cases which have been carefully collected by the Society for Psychical Research in London, which, as a whole, has always been disposed to doubt the existence of phenomena of a physical order but has recognised the indisputable existence of those of a mental order ; the latter have even been admitted by men of an essentially critical and skeptical turn of mind such as Mr. Frank Podmore and Dr. Hodgson. The deductions to be drawn from the existence of these supernormal faculties are as yet difficult to determine. It would, indeed, be premature to attempt to do so in an absolute and definite manner. But it is easy to see the exceptional importance which may be attached to them, since they tend to produce belief in an origin remote from our intelligence, and in an indefinite future in which they may be destined to find free exercise,—as our collaborator, M. Bozzano, has very finely attempted to prove, taking as his basis the law of evolution (ANNALS, September, 1906).

With regard to physical phenomena, these can all be classified as various degrees and forms of "materialisations." We may, in fact, suppose that raps and knocks, levitations and displacements of tables and other objects, with or without contact, etc., are produced by the liberation of the same force which produces what may be called "invisible, but tangible, materialisations," such as those which give touches in which the structure of a hand, or of some limb of the body can sometimes be clearly recognised, the plastic swellings of the curtains behind which one can feel, by touch, a human body, which, however, one cannot perceive when looking behind the curtains ; also visible materialisations, which can be photographed, but are not palpable ; those that are palpable or visible, but represent only a part of the human body, and finally complete materialisations.

Next come the apparitions of living beings at a distance. These apparitions in many cases, bear a character which suggests that they are subjective rather than objective. There are well authenticated cases of phantoms of living persons which have been seen simultaneously by different individuals ; and the person who was seen, has, for example, on awaking from sleep, declared that he was present on the spot, which he described, saying that he saw such and such persons and said such and such things—these details being subsequently confirmed by the percipients of the apparition. (Many of these facts may be found in *Phantasms of the Living*, by Myers, Podmore and Gurney.) In certain cases, the apparition is objective, material ; when it was capable of being touched, it has moved objects, knocked at the door, pulled a bell, or has been seen to write something which has remained in the hands of the percipients ; as in the famous case of Robert Bruce, which may be found in *Animism and Spiritism*, by Aksakoff, with other facts of the same kind.

The objection may be raised that all these facts are not equally well proved. Doubtless that is true. But since the *savants* who experimented with Eusapia have proved the most extraordinary phenomena, such as materialisation ; since two other *savants* have recently photographed the levitations of the medium Zuccarini ; since phenomena of the mental class are accepted even by investigators who still dispute the authenticity of physical phenomena

; it is impossible logically to reject as a whole the phenomena which Profs. Morselli, Foà, etc., have not seen, but which are not more extraordinary than those which they have proved, and which are authenticated by the same testimony as that which learned experimenters have recently shown to be worthy of confidence.

We may, in short, admit that different classes of metapsychical phenomena are true as a whole ; that it *seems* as if our minds possess marvellous supernormal qualities which seem destined to find exercise in an existence other than terrestrial ; that it *seems* as if "something" really emerges from the body of certain persons "as a snail emerges from its shell" (to use the simile by which the assistants of Prof. Mosso try to ridicule this hypothesis) ; and that these persons do not merely extend around them prolongations of their nervous or other forces, as a cuttle-fish extends its tentacles, if this elegant image expresses correctly the idea of these doctors.

Now, if you please, wherein lies the absurdity in the idea that these supernormal latent faculties, this "something," which Occultists have called the "astral body," and which I will be careful not to define, survives, temporarily or perpetually, its liberation from the body? Science—that science so profoundly ignorant that, ignoring all these phenomena, it does not possess any of the most important elements for passing judgments on these questions—can it, indeed, seriously maintain that it is absurd to admit thought without brain, when they do not know how these phantoms of the living can think without possessing a brain of their own? Is not this science joking when it proclaims, by the mouth of Marcelin Berthelot *"There are no longer any mysteries?"* Has it indeed come to this, that it pretends "to have extinguished the lights of heaven by a magnificent gesture?" (The magnificent gesture of the ostrich.)

And if this mind, endowed with supernormal faculties, if this body which has been called fluidic, or astral, survives, perhaps, its separation from the flesh, what is there that is absurd or impossible in the fact that it should attempt to communicate with the living, and, under certain conditions, should succeed? Spiritists, alas, constitute the heel of Achilles of spiritism; their lack of the critical faculty has thrown enormous and easily comprehensible discredit on "spirit messages." But their naive tendency to see the work of "spirits" in all phenomena which they cannot otherwise understand, their dull conversations with Joan of Arc and Melancthon, are no more an argument against the spirit hypothesis than the unguents of quacks, or than the innumerable mystifications of medical advertisements in the daily papers are an argument against medical science.

6. An Example of Cases Which Appear to Be Spiritistic

For, besides the absurd cases offered by spiritists, there are certainly some of a disconcerting kind. Let us quote one of the best known, as a means of elucidating our point: that of the daughter of Judge Edmonds.

Everyone is, no doubt, acquainted with this case: Judge Edmonds had a daughter in whom mediumistic faculties were revealed by the spontaneous phenomena which occurred in her presence, which soon aroused her curiosity to such an extent that she began to frequent séances. When another personality manifested through her she sometimes spoke different languages of which she was ignorant. One evening when a dozen persons were assembled in Mr. Edmonds' house, in New

York, a Mr. Green, a New York artist, was present, accompanied by a man whom he introduced under the name of Mr. Evangelides, of Greece. Soon a personality manifested through Miss Laura Edmonds, who spoke to him in English and communicated to him a large number of facts, tending to prove that the personality was that of a friend who had died in his home several years ago, a person of whose existence even no one present could ever have known. From time to time the young girl uttered words and entire phrases in Greek, which suggested to Mr. Evangelides to ask her if she could speak to him in Greek. He himself, as a matter of fact, spoke English with difficulty. The conversation was carried on in Greek on the part of Evangelides, and alternately in Greek and in English on the part of Miss Laura. Now and then Evangelides seemed to be much affected. The next day he resumed his conversation with Miss Laura after which he explained to those present that the invisible personality who seemed to be manifesting through the medium was one of his intimate friends, who had died in Greece, the brother of the Greek patriot, Mark Botzaris; this friend informed him of the death of one of his own sons, who had remained in Greece and was in excellent health at the time that his father left for America.

Evangelides returned several times to Mr. Edmonds' house, and, ten days after his first visit, he informed him that he had just received a letter announcing the death of his son; this letter must have been already posted when the first interview of Mr. Evangelides with Miss Laura took place.

"I should like," writes Judge Edmonds on this subject, "that someone should tell me how I should regard this fact. It is impossible to deny it, it is too obvious. I might as reasonably deny that the Sun shines on us... This happened in the presence of eight or ten persons, all educated, intelligent, reasonable, and all as capable as anyone of distinguishing between illusion and real fact."

Let us, however, make an effort in psychical acrobatism. Let us suppose that Evangelides had telepathically received tidings of the death of his son, and that this information had remained latent in his brain until the clairvoyance of Miss Laura Edmonds managed to evoke it, in connection with that which related to Mark Botzaris and all the rest. Still it would be illogical to attribute to the medium the gift of speaking the Greek language, and the knowledge of the death of the boy to two distinct causes, How came it that Miss Laura spoke Greek? The hypothesis that can explain this phenomenon has not yet been invented.

Mr. Edmonds informs us that his daughter had never heard a word of modern Greek up to that day. He adds that on other occasions she spoke as many as thirteen different languages, including Polish, Italian, Indian, whilst, in her normal state she only knew English and French—the other only so far as it can be learnt in school. And this J. W. Edmonds was not a nobody, far from it. He was President of the Supreme Court of Justice of New York, and President of the Senate of the United States. No one has ever thrown a doubt on the absolute integrity of his character ; his writings prove his brilliant intelligence. There is, therefore, no more reason for refusing to give credence to his accounts, so well authenticated, than to those of the savants who experiment with Eusapia Paladino and others.

Now, it is important to observe that, in this case the objection henceforth classical, cannot be raised, that in resorting to the spirit hypothesis the same intelligence is displayed as that shown by barbarians, who explain all the phenomena they cannot understand as due to spirit intervention ; and by the astronomers of the Middle-Ages, who attributed the movements of the stars to the guidance of angels, having no suspicion of the universal law of gravitation. A few months ago, speaking in this journal (vol. V., p. 295) of the phenomenon of the incombustibility of the medium Home (a phenomenon which even Mr. Podmore declares to be "the most difficult to explain and the best attested that has occurred with Home"), I remarked that as the medium's hair, his clothes, the objects and the persons to what he transferred his faculty became, in their turn, incombustible, we cannot reject, at least provisionally, the spirit hypothesis. This may be called reasoning like barbarians, if you like. But the case that has just been cited, in which the personality of the deceased person presents itself, gives its name, furnishes proofs of identity, is not similar. The investigator does not say that it is a spirit—the spirit of a particular deceased person—"because he does not know how the phenomenon in question is produced" ; he says so, not *a priori* this time, but through sheer force of reasoning: he thinks that identity has been proved ; his reasons are the same which make us say that so and so, and not someone else, has made a certain remark, when we speak of the living.

7. CAN THE SPIRIT HYPOTHESIS HE IGNORED IN THE STUDY OF MEDIUMISTIC PHENOMENA?

Can we and ought we to refuse to consider the Spirit hypothesis when studying mediumistic phenomena? It is not unusual to find that *savants* affirm that we should do so. These are men who are quite new to these studies, and who have never thoroughly examined the question.

It is natural to ignore all hypotheses when the physical phenomena of mediumship are being studied ; we confine ourselves then to verifying objective facts. But it is obvious that it is not equally possible to avoid examining the spirit hypothesis when we are considering certain mediumistic phenomena of an intellectual kind, for instance, when the attention is centered on establishing the identity of the personalities who are manifeasting. All the work which Hodgson, William James, Hyslop, Lodge, etc., have carried on with Mrs. Piper is based on that. We shall find in this same issue an article on the report made by Prof. Hyslop on his attempts to get into mediumistic *rapport* with his deceased friend, Dr. Hodgson. Evidently all the work done is based on the examination of the spirit hypothesis. Contrary, therefore, to what Prof. Pio Foà says in his recent address (ANNALS, vol. V., pp.442-9) a hypothesis is necessary in this case, and it is a legitimate, scientific hypothesis, a working hypothesis, which it is *impossible* to ignore. Can it be ignored in mediumistic phenomena of a physical kind? Yes, most certainly. But the physical phenomena of mediumship are never exclusively physical ; they are blended with intelligence, and should we not examine the spirit hypothesis in connection with the study of this intelligence, as well as in all other intellectual mediumistic phenomena?

8. Is the Spirit Hypothesis well established?

Now, can we say that the legitimacy of the Spirit hypothesis in certain mediumistic phenomena is definitely established?

Not at all ; far from it. Almost all savants, and the greater number of those who have studied the subject in a strictly scientific attitude of mind (others do not count) do not think so. For my own part, not only am I not convinced of the secure foundation of the spirit hypothesis, but I recognise plainly that I am tending further from, rather than nearer to, this theory. Why? Not for the trivial reasons cited by Prof. Morselli (on page 416 of the ANNALS for June, 1907), out of a work by M. G. Negri, namely that the nonsensical meanderings of the so-called spirits does not make this hypothesis appear either "consoling to our sacred affections, or flattering to our vanity," etc. For my part, such reasoning seems worth no more than the reasonings of those who think to convince us by asking us, for example, if we wish to put ourselves in the same class with the brutes, if it is not painful to us to think that after death we shall never be re-united with our dear ones, etc. The question is not what we *desire*, the question is, what *is*? In the same way, it is not to the point to bemoan that men, often not of brilliant intelligence in this life, do not acquire, *ipso facto*, the most valuable qualities after their decease, or that they should busy themselves in making tables dance instead of singing hymns around the throne of the Most High, like the angels in Milton's Paradise. Do not let us leave the experimental domain to entangle ourselves with metaphysics and theology.

From the experimental point of view, however, the

evidence which we have collected up to the present appears to me very insufficient. In particular, we do not understand why the evidence so far forthcoming is always fragmentary, filled with lacunae and entangled with error. These personalities of the deceased—who give sometimes astounding proofs of identity, revealing secret details of their lives, speaking just as the individual in question would have spoken in his lifetime, yet at the same time incapable of giving us the name of wife or child or other essential facts of the same nature, absolutely perplexes us.

We know the ingenious, and perhaps correct, theories by which it is attempted to explain these lacunae of intelligence in the persons supposed to visit us from the Beyond ; we refer to them in the present issue, with reference to the experiments of Prof. Hyslop, but we confess that we find some difficulty in accommodating our understanding to conditions of existence so different from those in which we live. Lastly we are obliged to recognise, with spiritistic writers themselves, such as Myers and Aksakoff, that we do not see how we can arrive at establishing, in a *positive* manner, the identity of a "spirit" ; and that we ought to limit ourselves to a relative certainty, such as we hold concerning historical truths, the social sciences, etc.

But, finally, can we seriously speak of the irrationality of the spirit hypothesis, of its anti-scientific character, etc., when what surprises us in metapsychical phenomena, taken altogether, is, on the contrary, that their rational connection does not more definitely convince us of the survival of spirit, of a body appearing to consist of a "fluidic" nature, which manifests in these phenomena ; what really surprises us is the difficulty which we experience in passing this last milestone on the road which our investigations have to pursue.

Moreover, why should we stick so obstinately to the spirit hypothesis properly so-called? We know that Sir Wm. Crookes, for instance, whilst he asserts that he has not been able to identify the so-called spirits as souls of deceased persons, at least declares that he is persuaded that they are spirits independent of the *psyche* of the medium. Flammarion closes his recent work, *Les Forces Naturelles Inconnues*, by saying that the study of mediumistic phenomena has not enlightened him as to the identity of the intelligences which manifest through mediums, but that they have led him to believe more than ever that:

1st, the soul exists as a real being, independent of the body;

2nd, that it is endowed with faculties as yet unknown to science;

3rd, that it can operate at a distance, without the intervention of the senses.

W. James, Lodge and a large number of other *savants* have come to about the same conclusion.

Under these circumstances, it can readily be understood that the question of the identity of the "spirits" may be regarded as a secondary question. What it is important to establish is the real essence of human nature, the well-foundedness of the materialistic or of the spiritualist hypothesis; but we must establish it experimentally, scientifically; we must solve the "riddles of the Universe," but we must solve them without ignoring the most important co-efficients which observation and experiment have put within our reach. And above all we must not rest satisfied with words. We do not solve a difficulty by saying, as Prof. Morselli does, that mediumistic phenomena are the product of *psycho-dynamism.* Spiritists also are "psycho-dynamists" ; that is indisputable. The important thing is to know how this psycho-dynamism enabled Miss Laura Edmonds to speak a language that she did not know, etc. I am altogether in agreement with M. Flammarion when he says that the spirit hypothesis should he sifted as well as the others, because, if its well-foundedness has not been proved, *neither has this been done with regard to the other hypotheses* ; on the other hand, discussion has not disproved it.

9. THE LIMITS OF AGNOSTICISM

Are our efforts in search of truth along this line of thought destined to arrive at something?

Why not ? A school of thought, of an *a prioristic* kind like most of the others, has been formed under the deceptive name of *Positivism,* which teaches us that science will never be able to solve the mysteries which lie beyond the tomb. This is, *par excellence,* a case in which to recall infamous Words of Arago: "*Qui, en dehors des mathématiques pures, prononce le mot impossible comment tout au moins une imprudence.*"

It is incontestable that science can never *directly* resolve abstract religious dogma such, for instance, as whether Brahma is really (as the Hindus claim) the first person of the Divine Trinity, an emanation of Vishnu and of Siva. Ought we therefore to refuse to regard this question scientifically? Do not let us jump to over-hasty conclusions! If science became capable, *verbi gratia,* of sapping the foundations of Brahminical Religion at those points which come within its domain, in proving the inaccuracy of its dogmas relative to cosmogony, etc., the most abstract dogmas, such as those concerning the Brahminical Trinity, would in their turn fall, *indirectly*, under the blows of science. Of this the "Positivists" positively never thought.

What is true from the *destructive* point of view may also be true from the constructive point of view. How many surprises of this kind science has already held in reserve for us! "It is evident," once said Arago, forgetting his wise counsels on the subject of the *impossible*, "that we cannot and never shall be able to know the chemical composition of a star." He said, in fact, that even if a fragment of this star should fall on our globe we should not know whence it came. The thing was indeed so *obvious* that no one thought of questioning it ; a few months later, however, the discovery of the spectroscope made it possible for astronomers to analyse the chemical composition of the stars. Kant had scarcely proclaimed the limits of the Knowable, when this genius, impressed by the phenomena of clairvoyance and telæsthesia presented by Swedenborg, was obliged to acknowledge that these facts and others similar to them would perhaps enable us some day to solve the mystery of that which seemed unknowable, and to prove that we live continually, without knowing it, in *rapport* with the world of spirits.

Ignoramus! We must say with Prof. Foà, but not, *Ignorabimus!* a word of arrogant humility. We ourselves are of those who have a greater idea of the mission and future of science ; we are not of those who point to the Pillars of Hercules and cry out to science, *Thou shalt go no further!*

10. The Future of Psychology

At present, all is still vague and uncertain ; we are still in the domain of chaos.

> *"De quel nom te nommer ; heure trouble où nous sommes? Rien n'est dans le grand jour, et rien n'est dans la nuit."*

"The age is in travail," as Victor Hugo says in *Les Châtiments*.

But in the course of a few years, since the study of metapsychical phenomena has been undertaken by observation and experimentation, more important, because more positive, results have been obtained than those reached by previous investigators, including official psychologists who were ignorant still of these phenomena, and who on this account alone belong henceforth to the past. Human nature has presented itself to audacious investigators in an entirely new light. The psychologists who have verified these phenomena and have known how to use them, will one day be seen to be as much in advance of their colleagues of yesterday and today, asastronomers who recognized the system of Copernicus were considered in advance of those who followed the old system of Ptolemy, however scientific they may have been in matters of detail. Under these circumstances, the indifference of a large proportion of the public and of *savants* towards these studies might naturally surprise us, if various conditions which have been already indicated by many writers, and which it is needless to repeat here, did not in some degree explain it. "They know not!" They will perhaps know soon, and they will not feel over proud of having been the last to recognize these scientific truths.

The import of the study of supernormal psychic faculties

will doubtless he considerable but we cannot yet say if, as Myers believed, it will amount to an *Instauratio magna* in the knowledge of the human being, from a scientific point of view. There are already strong reasons for thinking so. Let us hope that the doubt will soon be resolved ; it is perhaps, not the twilight of evening, but the dawn of morning, which is manifesting itself to our astonished gaze.

A Contribution to the Study of Materialisations

By Dr. Joseph Venzano
(Annals, Aug 1907)

1. Introductory

Those who study metapsychism have recently devoted special attention to the phenomenon called materialisation. This is a subject which must necessarily awaken suspicion, and suggest fresh criticism on the part of skeptics. It is not enough that these phenomena should be presented with prudent reserve, in a rigorously methodical manner, or under the protection of authoritative names. Skeptics incapable of this calm judgment, and without that competence which profound knowledge of the subject affords, relying chiefly on recent cases of mediums being surprised in flagrant acts of fraud, persist in their form or methods of negation, contesting the facts, depreciating without reserve the testimony of the witnesses, and generalising, after their usual manner, in their one-sided conclusions.

This is, moreover, only a repetition (in a milder form) of what has always happened. The act of proclaiming certain truths which go beyond the intellectual inheritance of any period, whilst it is a test of courage, also carries with it, unfortunately, a long train of disillusionments and bitternesses. There is nothing more dangerous than facing unpopularity. The man of science, even when he has contributed, by his teachings and by his marvellous discoveries, to create the glory of the age, if he ventures to assert some new fact which appears to contradict the known laws of biology, encounters the ungenerous and ill-considered indignation of crowds of detractors, who are always ready to deny not only the facts presented, hut even the scientific competence of the man who attests them.

This is the main reason for the prolonged silence of many eminent men, who no longer have any doubt as to the reality of mediumistic phenomena, the proclamation of which would entail upon them the risk of diminution of their authority and of the prestige attaching to their well-advised utterances. This is *a fortiori* the reason for the silence of those who, like the author of this article, are but obscure though conscientious investigators in the domain of metapsychical research.

This does not, however, alter the fact that it is the duty of those who possess rich material to bring their contribution of diligently accumulated and rigorously examined facts, when circumstances require that they should do so, and in view of the fuller preparedness for accepting new gifts of science which is at present apparent among the public.

It is with this object that, in view of recent discussion of phenomena of materialisation, I have decided to publish a series of very interesting occurrences, relating to this subject, which took place with the medium Eusapia Paladino ; I hope thus to contribute to prepare the way for these scientific truths, which in spite of the opposition of discordant opinion, are making steady progress, asserting at every step their sacred rights.

Before entering upon the detailed examination of

these mediumistic, which I am about to relate, I think it expedient to offer a few general considerations, which the character of the present article renders necessary.

The phenomena occuring with Eusapia constitute an assemblage of physical manifestations which *appear* to contradict the known principles of biology. I say appear to contradict, because no one can deny that these manifestations are connected with natural laws which are not yet within the domain of sciense. The proof of this statement may be found indisputably in the study of the marvellous discoveries in the domain of science, which have succeeded one another at short intervals, and which indicate how numerous and how important are the ideas which still remain to be acquired.

There is no need to cry "miracle!" every time we find ourselves in the presence of mediumistic phenomena. Miracle, moreover, is only an extraordinary fact which is opposed to that which we know by experience, or, to give a better definition, it is only the effect of causes at present unknown to us ; consequently it is not contrary to natural laws, but only to the limited knowledge of nature which we possess. Abnormal rnediumistic phenomena, therefore, as well as normal phenomena which come under our daily observation are the result of natural laws which are fixed and immutable ; laws which, however, are connected, each and all, with a primary cause of which we are entirely ignorant.

The first cause of the development of an embryo is as much unknown to us as that which precedes that assemblage of facts which results in materialisation. Nevertheless, the embryological development of an egg, simply because it is daily under our observation, is a fact which we are accustomed to call normal ; this is not the case with mediumistic phenomena, which only occur under exceptional conditions and cannot be reproduced at will.

These considerations, it will be observed, are in correspondence with the theory of *relativity of cognition*, which was maintained by Immanuel Kant. The positive school, in spite of the prodigious efforts made by its partisans, has been obliged to recognise that human investigations have limits, beyond which there exists what Spencer has called the "Unknowable."

The world, in fact, by virtue of the limited faculties of our senses, does not appear to us as it really is, so that we are only able to form a relative conception of it. It seems then as if human research must be arrested in front of these Pillars of Hercules which make the confines of an unknown world, the refuge of the science of reality, in which is indubitably hidden the solution of the mysterious problem concerning the Genesis of the Universe.

At this point we ask ourselves a question: "Can we say with Littré that this infinite ocean whose waves beat upon the shores of this island which we inhabit" is in no way navigable? Must we say that human effort must pause before this immense rock, considered up to the present as inaccessible?

Let us reply first with Taine: "Man sees the limits of his own intelligence, but he does not see the limits of the intelligence of humanity." Darwin also tells us that "it is always those who know little, and not those who know much, who loudly affirm that science can never solve such or such a problem." The late lamented Prof. Angelo Brofferio, even before the experiments made in Milan with Eusapia, had modified his positivist tendencies, speaking, in his fine treatise on psychology, of the possibility of scientific metaphysics, said: "It is presumption to believe that others may not be able to discover what we ourselves cannot discover. We can only say that we do not see the way in which to resolve the problems of metaphysics. But others may perhaps be able to find the way." And further on: "Who knows what we may learn by new instruments like the microphone by such new mathematical methods as analytical geometry and the infinitesimal calculus, by *new methods of observation such as psycho-physics and hypnotism?*" This is a notable prediction by this eminent psychologist, who, in certain mysterious activities of the mind, caught a glimpse of new horizons opening for science!

In truth the progressive and continuous succession of extraordinary discoveries, as well as the new and interesting results of experimental psychology, renders less arduous the road that may lead towards this goal.

To these considerations we may add another, drawn from the theory of evolution. Who can logically refuse to believe that, in the course of thousands of years, the intellectual faculties may develop to such an extent that at last they may stand in the same relation to human reason as the latter bears to the instinct out of which it has arisen? Knowledge drawn from anthropological research, and particularly from comparative anatomy, demonstrates also the possibility of modifications of substance in the living, thinking organism, which ceaselessly tends towards perfection, under the guidance of the inevitable laws of the struggle for life, of natural selection, amid adaptation to environment.

This is not to say that human intelligence must in the long run attain directly to the explanation of the mysteries of the unknown. We may suppose, rather, that by means of the general results obtained from different sciences some primary principles may be discovered, which will explain others (Brofferio). And when we remember that it is possible to deduce from a portion of a thing what the whole must be, and that by the aid of sight, the telescope, and mathematics, we can penetrate into the infinite depths of the heavens, the eventuality of this splendid triumph of human mentality seems undoubtedly possible.

Consequently, the notion of scientific metaphysics ought not to be in opposition to the methods of investigation of the positivist school, which *cannot refuse to admit* the possible existence of an initial cause of all causes, under the sway of which are unfolded the natural laws to which the whole of creation must conform.

Hence the importance, which up to the present has not been sufficiently recognised, of the study of metapsychism considered as a science which, by revealing faculties of the human soul which we have constantly ignored, may furnish new and precious elements for the interpretation of the enigma of life.

And now, having offered these summarised considerations, which reflect our opinion concerning the limits which knowledge may reach, we will enter directly upon the subject which we propose to discuss.

2. Presumed Forms of Materialisation

"Materialisations" may be produced eiter in complete or incomplete forms. The instances in which the materialisations assume the complete form of a living human body are very rare with Eusapia. The materialisations are generally those of partial forms, such as busts and human heads, limbs and portions of limbs, which are generally formed behind the black cloth curtains of the cabinet. Even when the human busts appear distinctly, the limbs are sometimes incompletely formed. These forms, in a very few cases, are perceptible to the sight in full light ; less rarely they can be seen in semi-obscurity when the room is dimly lighted by tinted lamps. Sometimes, on the contrary, on account of the darkness of the room, the form only manifests its presence by means of touch or hearing. Hands touch us, and clasp ours ; heads approach us so that we can recognise their outlines by means of touch ; voices are heard murmuring in our ears words of which we succeed in grasping the signification.

To these different manifestations should, in my opinion, be added that not less complex mediumistic phenomenon, in which the objectivity of the form which is in process of materialisation is not sufficient to permit the eye to perceive its presence, although, on the other hand, the manner in which the phenomenon develops makes it reasonable to suppose that it is there. To this category belong the phenomena of so-called transports which are so often observed in mediumistic séances, especially with Mme. Paladino, and which are accomplished as if directed and executed by a conscious entity, sometimes endowed with peculiar perceptive faculties, certainly surpassing those of the persons present, which enable it to execute, even in total darkness, complex movements of transport of objects, sometimes of considerable weight and dimension ; and also far out of the reach of the medium's hand.

The same applies to the phenomenon of imprints obtained on clay prepared for this purpose and executed under conditions such as to exclude all possibility of fraud. These imprints which, for example, reveal a face, a hand or a reasonable grounds for supposing that the face, or or the foot, of a materialised entity has come and impressed its shape on the clay.

These brief considerations, which we will presently

substantiate by irrefutable facts, lead to a very important which is: that a large proportion of mediumistic phenomena suggests the intervention of a conscious entity, who, whatever may be its origin, is able to objectivise itself in such a manner as to acquire the character of a anaterialised form.

We say "a large proportion," because there are phenomena, the manifestations of which exclude the necessity for their intervention, as for instance, the levitation of tables, which may result simply from a force of attraction, which may be liberated from the hands resting on it. One may also attribute to the effect of this force the movements of objects, even at a distance, which are executed in the direction of the medium, and are, as a rule, accompanied by synchronous movements on the part of the medium herself.

When proposing to ourselves to make a contribution to research into the study of materialised forms, we have not felt justified in neglecting that aspect of mediumistic phenomena which, as we have said, is associated with the supposition of the existence of an entity who may control and execute the phenomena. We have therefore with this object collected many cases, which will obviously prepare the way for the study of true materialisation.

Although the facts in question are relatively numerous, and many of them have been verified and attested by distinguished friends, we will, nevertheless, only quote certain quite typical cases which occurred in our presence, and came under our own direct observation, under such conditions of precaution as to render them unassailable by skeptics.

CASE I.—This is apparently a case belonging to the most simple class of mediumistic phenomena, but interesting nevertheless on account of the conditions of light and control under which it was produced. It occurred at a séance which took place recently at Genoa at the house of our friend, M. Alfredo Berisso, the distinguished Argentine artist, who was present for the first time at phenomena of this kind. The séance had been decided upon a few days. before, and M. Berisso had courteously confided to M. Ernest Bozzano and myself the preparation of the improvised cabinet. On the very evening of the experiment we chose M. Berisso's dining-room. After we had put seals to the windows (the apartments are on the fifth floor) we improvised a cabinet by attaching two curtains of black cloth to the hangings which covered the window recess, in which was placed a chair, and upon it a tambourine and a metallic trumpet which I had myself taken from among the toys of one of my children. The room, which at the time of the experiment was subjected to a strict and formal examination, was lighted by an electric lamp of sixteen candle-power. In front of the curtain had been placed a little rectangular table of white wood, and between this and the curtain itself stood the chair destined for Mme. Paladino. There were present at the séance: M. and Mme. Berisso, the artist, M. Francesco Brignola, M. Bozzano, Mme. Gellona and her son Ernest, myself and my daughter Gina. The control was entrusted to M. and Mme. Berisso. The part of the séance which refers to this first case is thus reported by M. Berisso himself:

> "When the séance had but just begun, and whilst the room was still lighted by an electric lamp of sixteen candle-power, a very important phenomenon was observed, namely, a trumpet was distinctly heard playing inside the cabinet, at

different distances from the ground, so that all heard it. Shortly afterwards M. Brignola called the attention of the experimenters towards the ceiling, where the trumpet appeared suspended in the air between the two curtains, and a little behind them, at a height of not less than a yard above the medium's head. It was placed transversely, with the opening towards the right side, on which I was seated, and the other extremity towards my wife, who had taken her place opposite to me and to the left of Eusapia. The hands of the latter were lying motionless on the table, controlled by ours, and perfectly visible to everybody. After a time the trumpet withdrew, and in retiring it again emitted various sounds several times."

The importance of this episode, carefully reported by M. Berisso, certainly cannot escape anyone, for, although it seems slight in character, it is nevertheless attested in a really exceptionally convincing manner. The phenomenon of sound and that of transport were in fact produced in full light, and everyone could see Eusapia seated, with her hands on the table, controlled respectively by M. and Mme. Berisso. Moreover, when the trumpet was visible in the air, it was at a height beyond the reach of the hands of the medium, as well as of those present. It is therefore natural to observe that, the intervention of the medium and the experimenters being excluded, the phenomena of transports and reiterated sounds of the trumpet can only rationally be attributed to the action of an entity, perhaps even partially materialised, and not perceptible because it was developed in the obscurity of the cabinet, an entity who performed neither more nor less than a living person could have performed.

CASE II.—*Séance of May 22nd, 1900*. Place: the rooms of the Minerva Club. The room in which the experiments took place communicates with an ante-room. The doors and windows of the room were hermetically closed and sealed. The cabinet was formed by the recess of one of the two windows of the room ; its front side consisted of a double curtain of black cloth, fixed at the top. At about a yard from the cabinet was a table of white wood ; between the latter and the curtain was placed the chair, on which the medium was to sit. On one wall of the room, at a distance of about a yard and a half from the medium, a guitar was suspended ; on a little table more than half a yard away from the medium was placed a typewriter (Columbia Barlock, No. 6), weighing 30lbs. Within the cabinet, on a chair, was placed a tambourine, surrounded by little metallic cymbals. Those present were: Profs. Morselli and Porro, Messrs. Avellino, Bantle, Da Passano, Ferraro, Peretti, Schmolz, the Countess Rey, and myself. The medium was at first under the control of Prof. Morselli, who was on her right, and Countess Rey on her left. The room was dimly lighted by a candle placed on the floor of the ante-room ; the control of Eusapia's hands and feet was rigorously maintained, and there was a succession of varied phenomena.

Towards the close of the séance M. Ferraro took the place of Prof. Morselli, whilst the latter went to the left of the medium, in place of the Countess Rey. At the same time the door of the ante-room was completely opened, so that the room was a little better illumined by the light of the candle. Under these conditions the episode occurred which I have related as follows in the report of these séances:

"The control was more strict than ever. The guitar suspended on the wall was heard to move. It was unfastened and carried in the air ; it passed round the table, rapped repeatedly on the head of Professor Porro, and finally stopped on the table. A little later it rose to the height of more than a yard, and again began hovering around the heads of the sitters before returning to the table. The tambourine which, as we have said, was placed on a chair in the cabinet, also moved. At one time the guitar rose up again, and moved about in the air *at the same time as the tambourine. This time the guitar went very high up, and it was distinctly seen crossing the room at the level of the top of the curtain (more than ten feet from the floor) followed by a streak of light, due probably to the reflection of the light of the candle coming from the anteroom and falling on the back of the guitar itself.* The control remained very strict. Suddenly a bulky object was heard to be placed on the table, and by the dim light it was seen to come from the corner of the room to the left of the medium. Dr. Venzano, who was at the end of the table furthest from the medium, was able to see this bulky object rise in the air, from the left corner of the room, pass over the head of Prof. Morselli and place itself on the large table in front of him. It was found that this object was the large No. 6 "Barlock" typewriter weighing 30 lbs. Soon afterwards the séance was closed on account of the lateness of the hour."

The incident above described is not less interesting

The Study of Materialisations

and is much more complex than the preceding case. We have not this time to deal with an isolated phenomenon of transport, but with a series of transports (some of which occurred *simultaneously*) and which took place promptly, with precision and with manifest intention. We note that all this took place by dim light certainly, but, particularly towards the close of the séance, in conditions which made it possible to distinguish not only the medium and the experimenters who remained motionless in their places, but the objects themselves moving freely about in the air.

But even apart from these conditions of light, and even if we were to admit the possibility that one or both of Eusapia's hands might have been freed, and also those of the sitters, one fact would still remain inexplicable: that of the guitar moving in the air and traversing the ceiling of the room at a height of nearly four yards from the ground, and consequently out of reach of anyone's hands, even if they stood up.

Equally inexplicable is the fact of the transport of the "Burlock" typewriter, weighing 30 lbs., from the little table in the corner behind Prof. Morselli to the table in front of him. This is inexplicable because, even granting that the medium, controlled by the Professor and by Dr. Ferraro, might (by substitution of hands) have liberated one hand, it would have been impossible for her, on account of the weight, to seize the machine with her outstretched arm and to raise it up, above the head of Prof. Morselli, so as to place it on the table before which he was seated.

It is out of the question to explain these manifestations by possible aid from strangers introduced in the room with the medium first, because of the precautions which had been taken by those present, and also because the presence of a strange person at the séance could not have escaped the observation of the experimenters.

In face of these arguments there only remains the supposition of an Intelligence, whether intrinsically belonging to the medium and sitters or not, from which and by means of which unknown forces are liberated which assume the task of executing the phenomenon, as though it were actually executed by one or more human personalities.

CASE III.—The incident which we are about to relate is perhaps one of those which has most impressed us. It consisted of simultaneous phenomena of levitation and transport. It formed part of a séance held on the evening of May 25th, 1900, in the already described rooms of the Minerva Club. The sitters were the same as in the preceding séance, with the addition of Captain Enrico De Albertis. The same precautions were taken. Prof. Porro who was on Eusapia's right, and Prof. Morselli, who was on her left, controlled the hands and feet of the medium. The room was dimly lighted by one candle placed in the anteroom. The séance began at 9 p.m. ; an hour and a half passed monotonously and with very rare occurrence of phenomena. But during the last half hour the séance became extraordinarily important on account of the phenomnena, which succeeded each other without interruption. It was towards the close of the séance that the characteristic manifestation here reported occurred.

"Suddenly Profs. Morselli arid Porro perceived that Eusapia had been raised, along with her chair, and carried up to a level above that of the surface of the table, upon which she re-descended *in such a way that her feet and the two front legs of the chair rested on the surface of the table, which was partially broken.* Meanwhile the medium moaned, as if intensely frightened, and asked to be put back with her chair on the floor, *but almost instantly she was carried up again, and this levitation lasted for some seconds, so that M. De Albertis and Prof. Porro, without preconcerted arrangement and with completely simultaneous thought, succeeded in placing their hands under the feet of the medium and of the chair.* Shortly afterwards Eusapia, still seated, redescended on to the table ; she was held by those to right and left of her, the chair was pushed or thrown down backwards on to the floor ; and the medium, seized by several of those present, whilst still moaning, was carried to the floor and seated again in her place."

The above is taken from the report made at the time, and we are glad to confirm it by a few brief remarks from Prof. Porro, in which this distinguished astronomer clearly expresses the impressions made on him by this incident. Referring to the levitation of Eusapia along with her chair, he writes:

"It was a moment of great anxiety and amazement. The levitation was accomplished without blow or shaking, swiftly, but not by jerks. In other words, if one wished, by dint of supreme distrust, to imagine that this result had been obtained by artifice, one should have to suppose a pull from above (by means of a cord and a pulley) rather than a push from below. But neither of these hypotheses will stand the most elementary examination of the facts. Paladino was actually drawn up and sustained in a position absolutely contrary to static laws, by an invisible force, inexplicable in the present state of our knowledge of physics."

This phenomenon, if calmly and strictly studied, whilst it excludes the possibility of any artifice whatsoever, gives occasion for considerations of much importance. The raising of Mme. Paladino cannot be considered as the effect of a push which she might have given to her own body, so as to raise it, together with the chair, above the level of the table so as to fall again on to the table, along with the front legs of the chair itself. The fall on to the table under such conditions would be abrupt, and the table, which was already half broken, would have gone to pieces.

The same remarks may be made concerning the second levitation, during which Captain De Albertis and Prof. Porro were able to pass their hands under the feet of and the chair. "The action of rising from the table, even more than that of leaving the floor," very aptly observes Prof. Porro, "denotes the intervention of a force extraneous to the medium: the latter would, in fact, have had to exert a force upon a base too weak to enable her to rise from it without breaking it by the effort."

But the marvellous part of the incident in question does not consist in this alone. The chair on which Eusapia sat, when it came down, rested its front legs on the edge of the table-top, and paused in this position, whilst only the hands of the medium were in contact with those of the persons on either side of her, producing a result evidently contrary to the laws of gravity. This state of things, which naturally occasioned a moment of justifiable anxiety, continued for some time, during which Eusapia occupied a position from which she must necessarily have fallen if some unknown force had not intervened, acting like a *vis a tergo*, sustaining Paladino and the chair.

It is important also to note the state of mind of the during the phenomenon, which took place independently of the expectations of the experimenters, and more especially against the will of Paladino, whose exclamations of very justifiable alarm at suddenly finding herself in such a perilous position we could all attest.

Is case also, therefore, it is logically necessary to suppose the intervention of an intelligence, not only directing the phenomenon but capable of developing a force by no means insignificant, both to raise the medium and to maintain her in this difficult position.*

> [During a séance in the rooms of the Minerva Club, on the evening of May 10th, 1902, at which were present Prof. Porro, the engineer and his wife, Cavaliere Adolfo Erba, and myself, a levitation of Mme. Paladino seated on her own chair was produced, in a manner analogous to that above described. The control was entrusted to Mme. Ramorino and myself. The door and windows were hermetically closed and sealed, and we were in complete darkness. The phenomenon was executed with extraordinary rapidity, and as soon as there was light we saw Eusapia, with the chair on which she was seated, transported on to the surface of the table in such a manner that the front and back of the chair occupied its very limited space. This time also, under the weight of Paladino and the chair, the light table was in danger of breaking, and the terrified medium begged earnestly to be taken down from it, which

was almost immediately done.

We have briefly cited this further case because, in addition to the fact that the same observations apply to it which we made with reference to the other similar experience, it has a special value of its own on account of its having occurred under those conditions of obscurity which so frequently afford a pretext for skepticism. On this occasion the complete darkness affords an argument entirely in favour of the genuineness of this mediumistic manifestation. It would indeed he quite absurd to suppose that Paladino could, under such circumstances, have carried herself and her chair on to the table by a shove given to her body and could have succeeded in occupying precisely the limited space afforded by its very small dimensions. Finally, we recall that another analogous case was recently reported by the eminent Italian physiologist, Luciani, in an interview with a representative of the *Giornale d'Italia*.]

CASE IV.—This last case of the first series refers to an impression on clay obtained during the course of a séance on the evening of February 17th, 1902. The séance was held in the rooms of the Minerva Club, and Mm. Avellino, Bozzano, Evaristo Testo, Luigi Montaldo, and myself were present.

I have had the opportunity of witnessing many phenomena of mediumistic imprints, but I have chosen this one because it has a character which is almost new, and because it was accompanied by very strict measures of control, excluding the remotest suspicion of trickery. In citing it I do not assume that I am stating anything new, because this phenomenon has already been described by

M. Bozzano in his work *Ipotesi Spiritica e Teoriche Scientifache*.

It is not, however, inopportune, in view of the character and purpose of this article, to relate it, using to some extent the words of M. Bozzano, to whom the control of Mme. Paladino was entrusted.

The arrangement of the room was the same as in the séances already described, and many phenomena had been already produced when the entranced medium, personifying "John King," announced that an impression would be obtained ; and at the same time urged the experimenters to first observe in full light the free surfaces of three blocks of clay which had been prepared for the purpose.

The light was turned on, and the attention of all of us was directed to the surfaces of the three blocks of clay, which were observed to be quite smooth and soft. Two of these blocks were on the medium's right, lying on a large table, the other was on her left, on a chair ; they were about two yards apart.

M. Bozzano, in describing the development of this phenomenon, expresses himself as follows:

> As soon as it was again dark, Eusapia held out both her hands towards me—I was next to her on the right—then, turning towards me, she placed her knees between my knees, and her feet between my feet, at the same time resting her head on my shoulder. At once the indications which usually announce good phenomena began to be manifested ; that is to say, the medium began to shake, to have spasms, to emit sighs and groans. There was no indication of synchronous or accordant movements... After a few moments

Eusapia's agitation increased ; suddenly, leaning her whole person heavily against me, she uttered in a weak voice her usual phrase : 'It is done.' The light was immediately raised. Of the three blocks two bore deep impressions. In both appeared the distinct and complete print of the sole of a foot. These feet formed a pair."

Our investigations did not stop here ; we examined the prints of the feet and we recognised that they in no way corresponded to the size of the medium's feet.

The reality of a phenomenon which took place under such conditions cannot be disputed. It is sufficient to know that the blocks of clay were previously examined and recognised as quite smooth ; that they were not on the floor but one on a chair and the two others on a large table ; that between the two blocks which were impressed there was a distance of about two yards ; that the impressions obtained did not correspond with the size of Eusapia's feet, and that, finally, the form of control exercised by M. Bozzano was really exceptional, in order to assign to this evidence the value of absolute certainty. When we add to these arguments the absurdity of the hypothesis that the medium might have taken off her shoes and put them on again, we have a further proof of the importance of what we have reported.

There is, therefore, no objection which can invalidate the genuineness of this mediumistic manifestation.

By excluding the hypothesis of fraud as a possible means of obtaining the impressions, we leave no other alternative than that of supposing the projection of energy from the medium capable of concentrating itself into a real materialised form, and of representing itself in the clay under the appearance of two feet which were not those of Paladino.

The attention of the researcher should be directed to the fact that the obscurity of the room evidently supports the genuineness of the phenomenon ; skeptics who are ready enough to make use of the usual arguments for discrediting mediumistic phenomena do not take account of this.

With the report of the above-mentioned phenomena, we have completed a series of phenomena which, so to speak, are preparatory to materialisation properly so-called. In these occurrences there is no objective proof that there has been materialisation of any sort ; but they imply the necessary supposition of the intervention of "something" which takes, if not a real plastic form, at least consistency sufficient to liberate energies, to oppose resistance, and to accomplish acts such as might be accomplished by, a human being.

And even in relation to the phenomenon of mediumistic imprints, which we purposely left until the last, the intervention of a plastic form, which bears all the character of a portion of a human limb, appears to be a logical necessity.

How then is produced and whence comes this aggregate of energy which results in the formation of more or less objective materialisations, which possesses the faculties of a living human being, and even yet more remarkable faculties?

The interpretation which in the present state of our knowledge of metapsychics would be most acceptable to science is the psycho-dynamic one (Ochorowicz). This would involve real psycho-physical projections, which, under certain fixed conditions, could be liberated from the medium, and contributed to by the experimenters who form a chain, so as to produce various phenomena, the chief of which would be materialisation.

But can we regard this explanation as always sufficient when we desire to apply it to the cases just cited? In this connection we should remember that the chief characteristic of mediumistic manifestations is their purposefulness ; that is to say, that they are conducted under the supervision of an Intelligence which guides and directs them. Now, if we could always or exclusively trace this purposefulness directly or indirectly to the medium, the hypothesis of Prof. Ochorowicz might be accepted unreservedly.

In the greater number of mediumistic manifestations and specially in those in which the phenomenon is displayed in connection with synchronous movements on the part of the medium, it is evident that the will of the medium herself cannot be considered as extraneous to the phenomena, whether this volition be a direct manifestation of her own thought, or the effect of suggestion on the part of the sitters.

In the phenomena above cited, on the contrary, the synchronism does not seem to be evident. Nevertheless the execution of the manifestations is accompanied by a special state of anxiety, of restlessness, and of fatigue on the part of Eusapia, as if she were making no slight efforts to assist in the production of the phenomena. In this case also, as we see, the supposition of the intervention of the will of the medium, with, perhaps, the contribution of the suggestive influence of the experimenters, might be admissible.

But there are phenomena in which, in our opinion, purposefulness on the part of the medium disappears completely. The third incident of the first series, that is to say the one relating to the levitation of the chair, together with Paladino, supports our assertion.

It is not logical to suppose that the will of Paladino could have contributed to the accomplishment of this levitation, that is to say, that she *could have willed* a mediumistic phenomenon which constituted a serious danger to her personal safety. The proof of this was afforded by the cries and the expressions of terror of the medium when she was brusquely transported, together with her chair, on to the broken and dilapidated table on which the chair only just rested with its two front legs. Neither can this desire be rationally admitted as operating in the experimenters ; for, to begin with, the mode of levitation was to them absolutely new and unexpected, and however legitimate their desire to have new and impressive manifestations, they would certainly not have thought of a phenomenon as impressive and dangerous as that which came under our observation.

This then is a case (certainly not isolated) in which the will of Eusapia, even under suggestion, can scarcely be put forward ; it is rather one in which a new and independent will emerges, which certainly does not support the hypothesis above cited, a will, the genesis of which constitutes, at least for the moment, one of the chief problems of psychology.

For ourselves we pause for the moment at this point, reserving the formulation of deductions and further considerations until we have set forth a second series of more complicated mediumistic incidents ; that is to say, those in which materialised forms make direct impression on our senses.

3. Materialisations Proper

We will now consider the most interesting and extraordinary phenomena of mediumship: materialisations.

Those of which the existence is recognised merely by touch are indisputably the most frequent ones. In most cases we are touched or grasped by hands which rest the flat of their palms on our shoulders, sometimes gently, at other times with playful violence ; which caress, or push, or slap us ; or by fingers which pinch our skin, pull our ears, or the flaps of our coats ; we perceive heads, apparently human, which approach our own, kiss our brows or our lips ; whole bodies which press against us, whilst two arms embrace us affectionately.

These bodies, which seem to be real human beings, or more often, parts of human beings, are most frequently perceived while covered by the curtain of the cabinet ; on some rare occasions, however, they are not protected by the stuff of the curtain, but show themselves directly, having the consistency of flesh. Less frequently our hands are directly carried by the medium to touch the materialised faces, both when they are covered by the curtain and when they are exposed.

Under these conditions it is sometimes possible for us to seize them. I myself succeeded in grasping a hand during a séance at M. Avellino's house in June, 1901. It was rather a large hand, with all the characteristics of a man's hand. I purposely pressed it forcibly with the object of retaining it as long as possible in my own. After a little while, although I did not cease to increase my pressure so as not to let go of it, the hand freely withdrew itself from mine, at a certain moment, as if its dimensions had been suddenly diminished.

Another characteristic feature of these materialised forms objectively recognised by contact, is that they can be observed in several places at the same time. Often, in fact many persons simultaneously report that they are touched as if there were two, three, or more of these materialised forms.

All these manifestations occur equally in darkness and in more or less dim light, and are generally accompanied by swelling of the curtain of the cabinet. When the light is more intense, the phenomenon recognised by contact is confirmed by sight. The forms, whether covered by the curtain or not, advance visibly, so as to enable their movements to be clearly distinguished.

Sometimes materialisations are indistinctly perceived by sight alone. These are dark profiles which often appear indefinite in outline and are seen in the semi-darkness of the room lit only by a very feeble light.

There are also cases in which the forms manifest neither by contact nor to the sight, but only to the organ of hearing. These are raps made on the table quite distinctly, either by open hands or by fists ; fingers drum on the surface of the table or of other pieces of furniture ; the sound of hands is heard chapping one against another as if applauding ; soft voices murmur in the ear.

We should add that the materialised figures do not always appear in the same form or of the same dimensions. The limbs are of various lengths ; the hands are sometimes large and robust as those of a man of Herculean constitution, at other times they are delicate and soft as if belonging to a woman ; sometimes they are tiny hands like those of children of various ages.

Equally various are the sizes of the heads whose presence we observe ; occasionally the hair may be felt, sometimes long, sometimes short, smooth or curly, sometimes more, sometimes less substantial ; at times the hair is plaited like a woman's, or long and falling over the shoulders. In other cases one may recognise the outline in relief of a face, covered by the curtain, or uncovered.

It is only under exceptionally good conditions of

harmonious environment that one can obtain these apparitions of phantoms in full light, of which—particularly on account of the high authority of the scientific man who observed and described this appearance—the phantom of Katie King is the prototype.

The apparitions which are obtained through the mediumship of Eusapia Paladino manifest as living figures which move and smile, giving kisses, the sound of which can be distinctly heard by the experimenters. These figures, enveloped in white drapery, partly issue from behind the curtain of the cabinet, in which Eusapia rests on a little bed, to which she is fastened by cords with many knots. The partial exhibition of these apparitions and the observations we have made (as we shall show later on) of the complete materialisation of visible limbs, lead us to suppose that these forms are not as a rule complete.

After this general summary of the facts relating to this extraordinary part of mediumistic phenomena, we come to the various cases collected in our second series; as before, we shall be careful to accompany each of these cases with remarks which we shall summarise at the close of the present article, in the form of general deductions.

CASE I.—We were in the rooms of the Minerva Club where the habitual measures of strict control were taken, as already described. Profs. Morselli and Porro, Marquis Da Passano, the Countess Rey, MM. Avelino, Bantle, Ferraro, Peretti, Schmolz, and myself, were present at the séance. The following incident took place at the close of the séance, that is to say, when the two gas lamps had been lit (one with an Auer burner) and the room was thus completely lit up. Eusapia, at about a yard from the cabinet, was seated before the table, her elbows resting on it, and her hands, still watched by those on either side of her, placed in *front* of her eyes to shelter them from the overpowering light. Only a few of those present were still seated. With this preliminary I will now give the details of the incident as they appear in the report of the séance made by myself, under date May 20th, 1900:

> "The Cavalieré Peretti having approached the curtain, be felt himself suddenly grasped by a hand which gently pressed his own. This hand, as everyone could see, came from the interior of the cabinet, keeping itself all the time covered by the curtain, and its form was distinctly recognisable under the curtain. This unexpected occurrence excited the curiosity of those present, who, in turn, offered their hands and received in the same way an affectionate pressure. Prof. Morselli, for the second time, and M. Ferraro, who until then had stood apart, put forward their hands at the same moment, but the desired phenomenon was not produced again. Dr. Venzano and M. Schmolz, who had approached the medium whilst the phenomenon was being repeated were able, whilst the curtain was swelled out, to turn their attention to the interior of the cabinet, which was entirely empty, except for the chair and the lump of clay, whilst outside could be seen the relief, formed by the texture of the curtain, of the hand which grasped those of the sitters."

For many reasons an exceptional value attaches to this case. First of all, the incident occurred in full light; secondly, it was produced when the séance had closed, that is to say, when we had no longer any reason to expect fresh phenomena. Then, as soon as the desire to see the phenomenon repeated was ardently expressed by the sitters, there was almost complete consent, a consent, however, which ceased when the demand was renewed simultaneously by Prof. Morselli and M. Ferraro, who had waited until the last.

This is a case in which the hypothesis of the intervention of the will of the experimenters seems to explain little, and to be in contradiction with the facts.

Can we say the same concerning Paladino?

We cannot find in her, either, traces of a directing will which might explain this manifestation. In fact, she remained obviously passive in the presence of this new phenomenon; she was indifferent to it, and was chiefly preoccupied with the excessive light which had followed the termination of the séance. There was, therefore, nothing in Eusapia's demeanour which could lead one to consider the phenomenon as directly emanating from her consciousness; this, however, does not entirely exclude the possibility that it may have resulted from unconscious suggestion.

Another consideration. We have seen that whilst the hand which grasped those of the sitters was put forward covered by the curtain, and everyone could observe its firmness and strength, the interior of the cabinet appeared to M. Schmolz and myself to be quite empty, except for the objects which had been placed there.

This is further evidence of the close connection existing between darkness and materialisations, a connection which decreases in proportion to the completeness of the harmony in the surroundings and among the experimenters. In the case in question the form, in order to materialise, required a dark spot, which when the two gas lamps had been lit could only be found in the interi-

The Study of Materialisations 69

or of the cabinet. The cloth of the curtain, arranged as we have described, offered sufficient conditions of obscurity for the accomplishment of the materialisation.

But we will return to this point in connection with the incidents still to be mentioned.

CASE II—This took place at a séance held at the house of M. Berisso on the evening of July 5th, 1905. M. and Mme. Berisso, M. Bozzano, Dr. Eugenio Gellona, myself and my daughter Gina were present. The same precautions were taken with regard to the medium and the room described in relation to the second case of the first series. Dr. Venzano was on the right, nod Mme. Berisso on the left, controlling the hands and feet of Mme. Paladino. The room was lighted by an electric lamp of sixteen candlepower. The following extract has been taken from the report made by M. Berisso:

> "At a certain moment, within the cabinet, in which a bottle full of water and a glass had been placed on a chair, a noise was heard, evidently caused by these objects being knocked against each other. Shortly afterwards we heard the sound of water being poured from the bottle into the tumbler, and almost at once the curtain was shaken and a hand covered by the curtain placed the glass of water on the table in front of Mme. Paladino. Meanwhile the left hand of Dr. Venzano and the right hand of Mme. Berisso were distinctly seen on the table, holding the hands of the medium. As soon as the glass had been placed on the table, Eusapia expressed a desire to drink. We did not think it advisable to let her do so, knowing by long experience that this

might result in nausea and vomiting. She persisted in her request and we still refused it.

Eusapia became nervous and excited. Suddenly the right side of the curtain swelled out and partly covered the fore-arm of the medium, which was controlled by Dr. Venzano. Shortly afterwards my wife, Dr. Venzano and I distinctly saw a hand and an arm covered by a dark sleeve issue from the front and upper part of the right shoulder of the medium. This arm, making its way above the free end of the side of the curtain which was on the table, seized the glass and carried it to Eusapia's mouth; she leaned back and drank eagerly. After that the arms replaced the glass on the table, and we saw it withdraw rapidly and disappear as if it returned into the shoulder from which we had seen it issue.

Dr. Venzano, who did not let the smallest detail of this phenomenon escape him, asked the sitters whether they also had seen the arm which seized the glass, issue from Eusapia's shoulder. My wife and I confirmed this fact. M. Bozzano, who sat at the end of the table opposite to that at which the medium was seated, agreed that, for his part, he had seen a black mass detach itself from Eusapia's shoulder, and shortly afterwards advance under the side of the curtain lying on the table; the arm ended in a hand of living flesh which seized the glass; he was at once seized with the conviction that this was a case of a double, and he was about to communicate this impression to those present, when he was prevented by the exclamation of Dr. Venzano. Mme. Venzano and Dr. Gellona, on account of the position which they occupied, were not able to observe the first part of this phenomenon. It should be noted that during the period of the production of the whole of this phenomenon, Eusapia's hands were under control, and did not cease for a single moment to rest on the table, visible to everybody."

In this case the connection between the will of the medium and the phenomena produced is remarkable ; it is a fact which Aksakoff would unreservedly have classed among animistic phenomena.

The materialisation, on this occasion also, took place in full light ; the harmoniousness of those present doubtless contributed to its success. It is to he noticed also that the curtain still has a certain effect in the development of the phenomenon. The hand, when it first placed the glass on the table, was entirely enveloped in black cloth ; later on, it appeared uncovered along with the arm, but only for a very brief moment, for it at once slipped into the space between the table and the curtain which lay upon it, so that the limb was almost entirely covered by this cloth. In this way the materialised form managed to keep itself to a large extent in the dark, a condition manifestly advantageous for prolonging the persistence of the temporary formation.

But there are many other points which arise from a careful analysis of this incident.

If in the case in question we consider the materialisation in connection with the imperative desire to drink expressed by Eusapia, we see how the Intelligence who directed the phenomenon, in order to attain its object, only did what was necessary to enable the medium to obtain her wish.

In fact, by means of her mediumistic faculties, there

was formed a right arm issuing, so to speak, from her right shoulder, and (it is worth while to observe) precisely at that point which corresponds to the shoulder-joint on which the whole limb turns.

It is a typical case of doubling, of a supernumerary limb, which, in our opinion, shows that the Intelligence to attain its end had resorted to an admirably-judged piece of economy, following the most direct and the most simple path and giving also a proof of the application of the law of economy of effort which controls the production of all operations.

Of this manner of proceeding on the part of the directing Intelligence, which strives to attain, without useless expenditure of force, an object proportionate to the conditions of the surroundings, the harmony of the sitters, and the mediumistic attitude (if the phrase may be allowed) on the part of Eusapia, we have had not infrequent proofs, as we shall see later ; and perhaps it is for this reason that the materialisations obtained through her mediumship are, in the majority of cases, partial and incomplete. Only under very exceptional circumstances, when there was necessity for complete materialisations, were human figures formed which we had reason to suppose were complete.

And now one last observation, which does not relate to the possible origin of the materialised form.

If the phenomenon observed in full light had been produced in complete darkness or in conditions of light which did not permit us to distinguish clearly the hands of the medium, which were under control and resting on the table, the impression we should have received, thanks to our constant thought of the possibility of substitution of hands, would very probably have been a suspicion of fraud. Now, If from what occurred in the light

The Study of Materialisations

we draw conclusions as to what may take place in many other cases which occurred in more or less complete darkness, we shall see how careful we ought to be before we curtly affirm that a suspected phenomenon ought, or ought not, to be attributed to fraud. It is a circumstance that should never be forgotten by calm and dispassionate experimenters when estimating the facts, and more particularly when they have to discriminate between real phenomena and those due to trickery, which, unfortunately, are not of rare occurrence in the history of mediumship.

CASE III.—This is taken from a séance which took place on the evening of December 27th, 1901, in the rooms of the Minerva Club in the presence of Prof. Porro, and the regretted author, Luigi Arnaldo Vassallo, Cavaliere Erba, M. and Mme. Ramorino and myself. The arrangements were similar to those already described. At the outset of the séance the control was entrusted to M. Vassallo, who was on the medium's left, and to Mme. Ramorino on her right. The phenomena began, and continued to be varied and interesting. Shortly before the occurrence which we are considering (at an advanced period in the séance) the arrangement of the chain was changed, in consequence of a typtologic request by the table, and I took M. Vassallo's place as controller, whilst Mme. Ramorino remained seated to the right of the medium. A white electric lamp lit up the room. We will now quote from the report:

> "At this moment there were fresh and repeated appearances of the child's hand, previously mentioned, above the head of Eusapia. It was a little hand, evidently a right hand, of the colour of pink flesh, with tiny fingers, somewhat long

and thin, which might belong to a child of seven years old. These appearances were so numerous that it was impossible to count them. The little hand sometimes showed the palm, sometimes the back. At times it was seen with the tips of the fingers upwards, at other times with the tips pointing downwards, and it often moved with a gesture of salutation. Sometimes it remained visible for a very short time, sometimes for about ten seconds. Dr. Venzano and M. Vassallo, who was seated on his left, got up, and without breaking the chain or the control, they bent towards the curtain, so that they were able to observe it at a distance of a few inches only. Dr. Venzano expressed a desire to be touched by it, and almost at once the little hand approached, with its fingers in front, and stroked his checks repeatedly, so that the doctor felt then a warm touch. At a certain moment, the little hand seized his nose and two fingers pulled it gently, then took the lobe of his right ear and pressed it with a certain amount of force.

"The medium was awakened. The little hand retired, and after a few moments it reappeared with another little hand, the latter being certainly a left hand. As they appeared, the two hands parted the curtains, then disappeared and reappeared several times. The phenomena ceased for about a minute, during which M. Vassallo and Dr. Venzano sat down again. Suddenly, whilst the medium continued awake, and kept her hands, visible to every one, on the table and under strict control on the part of those sitting next to her, on the right and left, the curtain swelled out, and a hand much greater in bulk and in dimensions

The Study of Materialisations

than that of Eusapia, and at the sane level as the small hands previously described, came out of the opening between the two curtains, seized the head of the medium and drew it violently backwards. The medium, alarmed, tried to free herself, and began to cry out for help to the sitters. But the hand did not let go of her head and continued to drag it forcibly backwards, as if to carry it into the cabinet. At a certain moment the hand withdrew but it reappeared almost at once, along with another hand. The two hands, like the former ones, by the disposition of their thumbs, were manifestly right and left hands and by the identity of their characters seemed to belong to the same person, this time apparently a man. Whilst Mme. Paladino cried out and protested, they seized her on both sides of her head, and continued to drag it backwards so that it twice disappeared into the cabinet and was covered by the curtain."

This incident is of extreme interest, not only because it was produced in full light, but also because it gave an exceptionally good opportunity of observing, and at a very short distance, the materialised forms, and particularly of feeling direct contact with some of them.

In the first case of this series we have already described a materialised form of a hand which, covered with the cloth, pressed in succession the hands of the experimenters. In the second case of the same series we observed the formation of a whole front limb, which seized a glass placed on the table, raised it, and carried it to the lips of the medium. Now in both instances, noting the movements executed and the force developed by the materialised forms, we reasonably come at once to the conclusion that the forms were endowed with a true and proper organisation equal to that of living human beings. This conclusion is much more strongly confirmed by the last case that we have recorded. In fact, under the conditions of light, time and distance under which I saw the little hand which touched and stroked me, I was able easily to appreciate its consistency and degree of heat. And when my nose and the lobe of my ear were seized between the thumb and finger of this hand, I was able to observe a pressure and a pull such as would be produced by the hand of a young child. This tepid warmth which emanated from the little hand, the movements of flexion and of extension, the opposition of the fingers, the pressure and the traction backwards exerted by them, afford very strong evidence in favour of our conclusions; that is to say, that the hand in question was a living hand, with a bony structure formed the framework, with the muscles, tendons, and tissues belonging to a hand, vivified by veins and lymphatic vessels, animated by a nervous system which imparted to it all the qualities of vital energy.

The second phase of the incident, although it was not observed by direct contact, also confirms our assertion; namely, the apparition of the two hands which repeatedly seized Eusapia's head, and dragged it into the cabinet against her will.

The force of traction liberated from these hands in opposition to the resistance of Eusapia (as Mme. Ramorino and I, who had control of her, can testify) also proves, indeed, that the hands which appeared (hands of a robust person and apparently those of a man) must also have been endowed with a complete organism, a conclusion to which we have already come, with more abundant evidence, with regard to the child's hands already described.

As we have seen, on two different occasions in this incident, the apparition of two hands simultaneously was obtained, having on each occasion the character of two hands belonging to a single person. The first pair of hands was morphologically different from the second, and both were different from Paladino's. Moreover, they issued from the opening of the curtain at a short distance from the medium, and above the level of her head.

This then was no longer, as in the preceding case, a possible instance of doubling, but it was a materialisation at a short distance; in a word, an externalisation of forces condensing into a plastic form, and very probably starting from the medium's head. It is worthwhile to recall at this point the fact that when approaching the hand to Eusapia's head, just at the spot (the left parietal region) in which there exists a bone-depression, the result of a bad wound of ancient date, all the experimenters perceived a sensation like that of a current of cold air—a fact which makes it reasonable to suppose that this zone in the cranium of the medium may be a means of exit for the psychic energy.

We have now only to enquire whether there is a probable connection between these manifestations and the will which directed their production. It does not seem as if we could exclude all connection between the child's hands and the intention of the medium and also that of the sitters. It is even certain that the desire for such an apparition was very strongly felt by some of them. The same cannot, however, be strongly argued with regard to the apparition of the hands which seized Eusapia's head and succeeded in dragging it behind the curtain. In this case we can even distinguish two opposite wills, of which the will opposed to Eusapia's prevailed. This circumstance recalls the third episode of the first series, with this difference, that in the latter there were two wills opposed to each other, whilst in this case there is manifest contradiction of wills and a trial of strength as well.

CASE IV.—We will now relate two episodes which were observed in two séances held at different times, with the same experimenters, in the same place, episodes connected together so closely that they can be treated as one case. They have already been published by the lamented L. Arnaldo Vassalo, in his work *Nel Mondo degli Invisibili*. I think it is, however, desirable to reproduce them, both because I was able to follow them carefully during their manifestation, and because they pave the way for deductions which are very opportune for the object of my article.

The séances took place in the rooms of the Minerva Club, in the séance room prepared as for the preceding case. In the séance from which we take the first incident (December 18th, 1901), Mme. Ramorino was on the left and M. Vassallo controlled on the right of the medium. On the right of M. Vassallo were, in succession, myself and the engineer Ramorino; on the left of Mme. Ramorino were Prof. Porro arid Cavaliere Erba.

We now proceed to quote the report of the séance which I drew up myself.

"When the room had been darkened, M. Vassallo felt himself seized from behind by two arms, which embraced him affectionately, whilst two hands with long, thin fingers pressed and caressed his head. Meanwhile a head, apparently belonging to a young person, approached his face and kissed him repeatedly, so that those present could distinctly hear the sound of the kisses. Whilst the phenomenon was being produced the head of Eusapia, who was completely entranced, rested upon the right shoulder of Mme. Ramorino.

"M. Vassallo asked the name of the entity who manifested, and at once the table began to move, and gave by typtology the word Romano. M. Vassallo then remarked that this was one of the three names of his only son, usually called Naldino, whom he had lost a few years before, when he was barely seventeen years of age. He added that this name was unknown even by some of his near relatives.

"He continued his interrogations. Having asked for a proof of identity, a finger passed inside his jacket and rested against his inner pocket, in which, said M. Vassallo, there was a pocketbook containing the portrait of his son.

M. Vassallo persisted in asking for more complete evidence, and if it were possible, a visible manifestation. The table replied affirmatively and by typtology asked that semi-darkness might be made, which was done by placing a lighted candle on the floor of the anteroom adjoining. In this way a very feeble light was produced, but sufficicint to make it possible to distinguish the faces of Mme. Paladino and the experimeinters. Eusapia, still in a state of profound trance, kept her head, as before, resting on Mme. Ramorino's shoulder, Suddenly Dr. Venzano, who was seated almost opposite to Mme. Ramorino, saw a vaporous mass rise between her and Eusapia ; it was of an oblong form, gradually condensing at the top into a pear-shaped formation of the size of a human head, on which appeared successively a very abundant growth of hair, and the eyes, nose and mouth of a human face. Dr. Venzano, in order to assure himself of the phenomenon, got up, and was about to communicate his impressions, when Cavaliere Erba and Professor Porro, who were beside Mme. Ramorino, exclaimed at the same time: "A profile, a profile." Vassallo, who, in expectation of the apparition of a materialised form, was looking towards the back of the room, which on account of the light coming from the ante-room was somewhat better illuminated, turned towards the cabinet and was also able to see the head, which advanced repeatedly over the table in his direction, and then dissolved. The small white electric lamp was lit up. Dr. Venzano traced with a pencil on a piece of paper, a sketch representing the form he had seen, and at the same time M. Vassallo, who was very clever at drawing, reproduced with much accuracy the head in profile of his lost son. Then he showed the photograph in his pocket-book to those present. The points of resemblance between the face which appeared, the sketches drawn by M. Vassallo and Dr. Venzano, and the portrait in M. Vassallo's possession, were then recognised with lively surprise. In fact, the outlines of the head and its pear-shaped aspect, produced by the very abundant hair, above an oval face with the thinness of youth, corresponded marvellously. M. Ramorino, from his position behind Dr. Venzano and M. Vassallo, both standing, and consequently shutting out his

The Study of Materialisations 81

view, declared that he had not seen the apparition. Also Mme. Ramorino, seated somewhat on one side and in front of the apparition, said that she had not observed it either."

The second incident is not less interesting. It occurred at a séance held a few evenings later (December 26th). This time also the control was entrusted to Mme. Ramorino and M. Vassallo, with the difference that M. Vassallo was on the left and Mme. Ramorino on the right of the medium. On the left of M. Vassallo were seated in erder, Dr. Venzano and the engineer Ramorino ; on the right of Mme. Ramorino, Prof. Porro and Cav. Erba.

The incident took place when the séance was already far advanced, and it is reported in the minutes of the sitting as follows:

"At a certain moment (we were in total darkness) M. Vassallo said that a hand, which seemed to be that of a young person, was stroking his right cheek caressingly. He asked if it was the hand of Naldino, and the table replied in the affirmative. He then expressed a desire that Naldino should find upon his person an object which he had much cared for while he was living. Soon he felt that a pin was being taken from his cravat ; this pin was a present from the artist, Ernesto Novelli ; it belonged to his son (Naldino) and was prized by the latter. M. Vassallo had put it on that evening with the wish that it might be taken off by the entity when manifesting. He expressed his thanks, and persisted in asking for yet stronger evidence of identity.

"Then he suddenly felt himself seized under the armpits by two hands, which lifted him up, obliged him to stand upright, and drew him about two paces outside the circle and behind his own chair; that is to say, more than a yard away from the medium.

Under these circumstances M. Vassallo, in order not to loose the hand of the medium, passed it from his right hand into his own left hand, in contact with that of Dr. Venzano, so that Eusapia, remaining motionless, was under the vigilant observation of three controllers.

"Then M. Vassallo felt a human body, of about his own height, leaning on his left shoulder, and a face which, in his opinion, had the character of that of the deceased Naldino, remained for some time pressed against his face. He then received repeated kisses, the sound of which everyone could hear, and, meanwhile, broken sentences were heard, uttered in a soft voice, which replied to the repeated questions of M. Vassallo. Dr. Venzano, getting up without abandoning the control, advanced in the direction of the voice and succeeded in hearing several words pronounced in the Genoese dialect, among which were these words: *Caro papá.* The conversation between M. Vassallo and the entity lasted for some time, until, after the sound of a kiss, Dr. Venzano succeeded in catching this sentence: *Questo è ber la mamma.* (This is for mamma.)

"Almost at once the materialised form disappeared and the table requested, by raps, that the light might be raised. As soon as the white electric lamp had been lit there was seen advancing towards M. Vassallo, who was still standing up, a human form enveloped in the curtain of the cabinet, which embraced him whilst a hand, also covered by the curtain, seized that of M. Vassallo and held it for some time.

"The medium remained all the time motionless on the chair, her hands in contact with those of the controllers."

In these incidents are collected, as we see, the principal modes of manifestation of the materialised forms. We have in succession manifestations of a tangible, visible and audible nature. Some of them are developed in full light, some in complete darkness, or at least, in very feeble light. Those produced in full light are indisputable ; as to the others, it is desirable to submit them to careful and critical examination in order to be assured of their genuineness.

One of the objections which skeptics might oppose is that of possible sensorial hallucinations. But the hypothesis of hallucination, if we consider the phenomena attentively, will not stand the result of sane criticism. I was in the full possession of my mental faculties, and, as usual, free from all prepossessions, when my attention was attracted by this vaporous mass which, in condensing, gradually assumed the character of a human head. Nevertheless, I prudently waited before expressing my impressions, and it was not until I was completely convinced that I was about to express them, when I was forestalled by the simultaneous ejaculations of Prof. Porro and Cavaliere Erba, then by that of M. Vassallo. Moreover, the human form of the face which appeared against the dim background appeared to the witnesses in various conditions of perspective according to the positions they occupied. To Prof. Porro and Cavalier Erba, who were situated beside Mme. Ramorino, and consequently also by the side of the apparition, the latter appeared in profile ; to M. Vassallo and to me, who were in front of it, it appeared on the contrary as a full face. The fact that this was not an hallucination is confirmed also by the agreement with which everybody recognised the resemblance which the face perceived bore to the sketches drawn by M. Vassallo and Dr. Venzano, and also to the portrait in the possession of M. Vassallo, and which was quite unknown to us.

All these facts afford indisputable proof of the genuineness of the visual phenomenon observed.

Similar remarks might be made relative to the genuineness of the auditory manifestations which accompanied the second incident. Not only were they confirmed by those precent, but I was able myself, by approaching M. Vassallo, who was conversing with the materialised form, to catch several words and one complete phrase pronounced in Genoese dialect. Now these words could not come from the medium (even on the hypothesis of ventriloquism), first because of the direction from which the words came, then because I, who heard even one complete sentence distinctly pronounced ; and more particularly M. Vassallo, who kept up a long and animated conversation, recognised that in the low speech of the entity there was no trace of the characterisric accent which is usually found among Neapolitans, whilst on the contrary, the accent was typically Genoese.

Having thus shown the genuineness of the case in all its details, we will see what conclusions may be drawn from it.

We observe, in the first place, that the entity which manifested alluded to circumstances unknown to all present except M. Vassallo ; I refer to the fact of the portrait enclosed in the pocket-book, to that of the pin which he had intentionally put in his cravat on that evening, and to the typtologic communication of the name "Romano."

Now the mediumistic revelation of these circumstances, unless we are prepared to admit an actual appearance of the deceased, implies necessarily a transmission of thought,*

> *[Professor Morselli, in his synthetic exposition of mediumistic phenomena obtained with Eusapia Paladino, which appeared recently in the Milanese journal, *Corriere della Sera*, and in the ANNALS for May and June, alludes to several cases of transmission of thought which I collected and discussed in an article published in the ANNALS for January, 1906, observing that they are, in his opinion, rather probable than proven.
>
> In spite of the respect due to the authoritative utterances of the illustrious professor, I do not, however, find it possible to agree with him. In the series of facts of transmission of thought which I presented there were a few which might, taken by themselves, have been explained by the hypothesis of possible coincidence. There were, however, many others in which transmission of thought seemed obvious and indisputable, such as the case of M. Ferraro, who, having mentally expressed the desire that a ten-centime piece should be taken out of the pocket of his waistcoat and given to Professor Morselli, seated at a distance of more than three yards from him, obtained the prompt execution of the action thought of. The same applies to the case of Cavaliere Erba, who—Professor

Porro alone being in his confidence—having mentally requested of the entity (the so-called spirit of "John") to give him an antique coin, which he had hidden in a part of the room before the arrival of the medium, and beyond the reach of her hand, and at the same time to embrace him, the phenomenon was carried out with marvellous precision.

In the presence of these and other similar facts, any doubt with regard to the transmission of thought is devoid of reasonable basis, and, moreover, these absolutely convincing facts give great value to the evidence for transmission of thought, even in those cases which might, if considered separately, be attributed merely to coincidence.]

(*cont.*) the idea of bio-dynamism it lends itself to a double supposition: either that the will of M. Vassallo, intensified by the hope of seeing his son, was perceived by the subconsciousness of the medium (in a state of profound trance) in such a way as to provoke in her an externalisation of energy capable of bringing about the phenomena obtained ; or that the special faculties of her subconsciousness penetrated directly into the contents of M. Vassallo's mind and translated this into action.

But if we pause at this point to consider with some attention the mode of development of the manifestation obtained, we shall see that, if the will of M. Vassallo was able to co-operate in effecting it, this does not, however, exclude the possibility that another will may have intervened, the origin of which may have been either in the medium or external to her. In fact, the existence of an autonomous will, independent of that of M. Vassallo, appears first in the contents of the typtological reply.

There is no doubt that M. Vassallo, when questioning the entity, was moved by the desire to obtain the name of his son ; but, as he afterwards declared, he did not expect the name "Romano" in reply, this particular name being unfamiliar to his intimate friends, and even unknown to most of them.

This already indicates that a foreign autonomous will had intervened during the development of the phenomenon, choosing, independently of the volition of M. Vassallo, the least known name of his son Naldino.

But there are considerations of much greater importance in favour of this autonomy.

With regard to the materialised forms which appeared during this incident, we shall observe that they also were not among the phenomena desired by M. Vassallo. We recognise in them, however, a directing intelligence which could not be that of M. Vassallo. The repeated requests made by typtology, sometimes for full light, sometimes for complete darkness, sometimes for dim light, also show the intervention of an autonomous will, the origin of which the partisans of the bio-dynamic theory would look for in that subconsciousness which is considered to be the centre of psycho-physical activity in the medium. This psycho-physical activity is held to show itself in that assemblage of extraordinary effects with which mediumistic phenomena abound, and is regarded as being endowed with creative faculties capable of perfectly reproducing the appearance of a living organism. And in fact, in the case referred to, we should not only have had the manifestation of thought, but also the material reproduction of the object of thought, even with all the characteristics of human personality, identity of physiognomy, and actual correspondence! It is not inappropriate to observe that such an interpretation, on the basis of psycho-dynamism, is not less extraordinary than the transcendental hypothesis.

Another circumstance worthy of being considered in this case, is the fact that I was able to follow with extreme attention and complete calmness of mind the commencement and development of the materialisation. The passage of the fluidic mass, so to speak, to such a state of condensation that it took the consistency of a human head, endowed with all the properties of the head of a living person, occurred in a very brief space of time, and the dissolution of the form was also very rapid.

This manner of proceeding, moreover, is not disconnected from that noted by other observers, and leaving out of count the numerous cases not substantiated by absolute conditions of control, it is not out of place to recall the classical case of "Katie King," described by Sir William Crookes.

As to the original source of the matter necessary for giving consistency to the plastic form, we may be sure that it should be sought for in the medium. That the medium does indeed contribute to this in large measure has been experimentally demonstrated by Crookes (with Home), by Lombroso (with Eusapia), and by others in connection with diminution in the weight of mediums, examined before and after a séance ; absolute evidence was obtained in the case of partial dematerialisation of Mme. D'Esperance, a phenomenon reported and carefully discussed by Aksakoff.

With regard to the contribution of material substance made by the experimenters it cannot be positively asserted, although it may be to some extent conjectured. The various results obtained by dynamometric experiments upon them before and after a séance (Morselli) are evidently not very convincing, if we take into account the natural exhaustion following upon the psychic hypertension of anyone who makes an effort of attention, sustained sometimes for several hours. We have remarked above with regard to acoustic phenomena, that the words uttered by the materialised form were pronounced in a low voice. This is a peculiarity that we always observe with Mme. Paladino, and which, from what we have been able to learn, was always attested by all the experimenters (Lombroso, Morselli and others) who have held séances with the Neapolitan medium. I think that the reason for this peculiarity is associated with the fact, which I have already pointed out, that through the mediumship of Eusapia we very rarely obtain complete materialisations. The toneless voice is therefore in our opinion the necessary result of an organism not altogether complete.

If, to confine ourselves to cases beyond suspicion, we refer to the example of Katie King, we shall see that, being completely organised to such a degree as to be able to walk about in the light and to permit Sir William Crookes to feel her pulse and to listen to the beating of her heart, she conversed freely and at length with him in a voice which had the clear tones of a human voice. This affords evidence of a mediumistic potentiality indisputably more accentuated in Florence Cook than in Eusapia ; whence we deduce that the mediumship of Eusapia (except in rare cases) would seem not to be sufficient to produce complete materialisations. And it is on account of the relative insufficiency of her faculty that the plastic phenomena with Paladino reveal a tendency on the part of the directing intelligence to utilise all sorts of more direct and convenient methods for attaining the end in view.

Thus, in the present case, the form, materialised by a scanty light and unprotected by the curtain, appeared partially visible (figure of a human head) in full darkness still unprotected by the curtain, it presented itself as the complete figure of a man, and the same was obtained in a distinct light, when the curtain which enveloped the form constituted in itself a darkened space. This affords another very evident proof of the connection between darkness and mediumistic phenomena.

From what we have said there results, therefore, a series of inferences which we may sum up in a formula which, in our opinion, represents one of the constant laws which govern materialisations, and which may be expressed in those words:

The conditions which regulate the production of materialised forms, equally with the mediumistic force, are in direct proportion to the harmoniousness of the surroundings and in inverse proportion to the light.

CASE V.—Although very important in relation to myself this case does not attain the value of the foregoing, because it largely escaped the observation of the other sitters, and therefore rests almost entirely on personal impressions. It is, however, worth quoting, because, without prejudice to our final conclusions, on the one hand it confirms certain considerations with regard to the last case, and on the other it gtves rise to new ones which will receive further confirmation in the subsequent episodes.

This also took place in the rooms of the Minerva Club, with the usual arrangements as to the methods of control. The séance was held on the evening of December 29th, 1900, there being present, besides the writer, Profs. Morselli, Porro and Risso, M. and Mme. Ramorino and Cav. Erba. The medium was in contact by her hands and feet, to the left with Prof. Porro, to the right with myself. When the present incident occurred, the room was illuminated by the feeble light of a candle placed on the floor of the ante-room. The following account is from the minutes of the sitting.

> "Suddenly Dr. Venzano, who held the medium with his left hand, she resting her head, visibly to all, on the shoulder of Professor Porro, saw forming to his left, at about a hand's breadth from his face, as it were a globular, vaporous, whitish mass, which condensed into a more decided form, that of an oval, which gradually assumed the aspect of a human head, of which the nose, the eyes, the moustache, and the pointed beard could be distinctly recognised. This form came and touched his face, and he felt a warm and living forehead press against his own and remain there for a second or two. Then he felt the contact of the whole profile of the face against his own, with a pressure as of a caress, then the imprint of a kiss, after which the mass seemed to vanish into vapour near the curtains. The other sitters, meanwhile, were only aware of a vague luminosity in the direction of Dr. Venzano but they distinctly perceived the sound of the kiss."

This incident, being insufficiently supported by direct observation on the part of the other sitters, might easily give rise to suspicion of hallucination. This, however, I think should be promptly excluded. My mind, at the moment of the phenomenon, was not otherwise occupied than in a calm and objective contemplation of facts. Moreover, if we accept the hypothesis of a sensorial illusion, I should have been a prey to a threefold hallucination, visual, tactile, and auditive, the last being also shared by the other experimenters ; all these circumstances certainly do not strengthen the hypothesis of hallucination.

At this point I ought to add that the vaporous mass which condensed into the form of a human face with very pronounced features only remained visible to me for a very few moments, since it almost immediately came into direct contact with my own face, thus preventing me from using my visual faculties. But the impression of contact lasted longer than that of sight. This was maintained for more than a minute, and was for me of exceptionally objective reality.

And here, in deference to the truth, I must declare that both of these impressions permitted me to perceive with great precision the physiognomic characteristics of the face which appeared to me, and to recognise the extraordinary resemblance it bore to that of a very near relative whom I had the misfortune to lose a few years ago. I must also declare that, in the state of mind already mentioned, these details of identity were neither expected nor in my thoughts ; and that on seeing the vaporous mass appear and condense, M. Vassallo being present, I thought that it was a repetition of the phenomenon of apparition in which, at the previous sitting, M. Vassallo had recognised his own son.

As will be seen, the present case has very decided points of analogy with the fourth case of this series, and lends itself to similar inferences. There is, however, a notable difference as far as regards the search for the will directing the phenomenon. In the fourth case we have predominantly the will of M. Vassallo, who was animated by the intense desire of seeing his son again ; in the present case my mind was in a state of absolute passivity, and only when the phenomenon commenced did my thoughts turn to the probable appearance of a materialised form which was quite different from that which really appeared.

As to the subconsciousness of the medium, who in both cases was in a profound state of hypnosis, if in the case of Vassallo it may be considered to have acted under the stimulus of a powerful volitional impulse, this stimulus evidently did not exist in the case which concerned myself. In this latter case, either the mediumistic effects which proceed from her are consequent upon a will which is neither her own nor that of the experimenters, or else we are compelled to recognise in her subconsciousness, not only the extraordinary power of externalising a psycho-physical activity capable of organising a form, but also that of penetrating into the mental substratum of the sitters, and of calling forth the impressions of images stored up in their brain-centres and existing there in a latent state. But I shall speak of this in the light of data more important still than those of the present case, and contained in subsequent incidents.

To complete the observations already made, it may be useful to mention that the deceased person whose semblance I recognised in the materialised form which appeared to me had not been known during life either to Eusapia or to the sitters, and that neither she nor they had had the opportunity of seeing his portrait. This circumstance is of special interest, and we shall avail ourselves of it in our general conclusions in reply to the opinion of those psychologists who hold that Mme. Paladino's phenomena are the result of a special determinism, the origin of which is to be sought in habit and practice.

CASE VI.—The incident we are about to describe is taken from a sitting which took place on the evening of June 16th, or, in the dwelling of the Avellino family. The account this sitting is given in full in M. Bozzano's well-known book, *Ipotesi Spiritica e Teoriche Scientifiche*. The phenomena of materialisation therein described are numerous, and all of them highly interesting. To avoid excessive repetition, I have selected the one which most directly concerns myself and which has the clearest bearing on the subject of this article. By referring to the book named, the reader can form an adequate idea as to the importance of the incidents omitted, and convince himself that they strongly corroborate the inferences arrived at from the few now given.

All necessary precautions with regard to the surroundings had been taken by M. Bozzano and myself, at the request of the other sitters. The dining-room was selected as the place for the experiments, and for the sake of ventilation it was left in communication with a small adjoining room from which it was separated by a narrow passage. No cabinet was prepared, neither were the many objects placed near the medium which usually form the paraphernalia of séances.

The group of experimenters was composed of MM. Avellino, Montaldo, Morando, and myself, all members of the Minerva Club, together with Mesdames Avellino, Montaldo, Chiti, and the Countess Rey ; all persons capable of contributing to that harmony which is the essential condition of the successful issue of a séance. We all sat round a large table, at one end of which was Mme. Paladino, who at the moment when the incident took place was under the control of M. Montaldo on her left and of M. Bozzano, beside whom I sat, on her right. The room had been darkened, but not completely so, for a gleam of light from the street (we were on the third floor) shone through the window, and a very feeble light also penetrated from the passage communicating with the adjoining room of which I have spoken above.

With this preface we come to the narration of the actual incident as recorded in the minutes by M. Bozzano:

> "To my left and a little more than a yard away there was a small door, through the opening of which a faint light penetrated. Suddenly the hands of 'John,' laying hold of my temples, forced me to turn my head in that direction. I understood that the action was done with a purpose, and I redoubled my care of observation. Very soon I noticed, low down, something like a kind of black cone with uncertain, smoky and changing outlines. It seemed as if this little mass gradually condensing in front of me were animated, or rather convulsed with a rapid rotary motion. It rapidly increased in size and length until, in a few moments, it attained the height and size of a man. Then, in less time than I can tell it, I was aware that this form had assumed the aspect and profile of a human being. This form was not more than two paces from me. My companions all noticed that the light from the doorway was unexpectedly and almost entirely obscured. Our sensations therefore coincided and supplemented each other.
>
> "Mme. Paladino at this point raised my hand and carried it in the direction of the form. Immediately two other hands took possession of mine, and carried it upwards. I then felt a soft, long beard, which passed and repassed over the

back of my hand, causing a tingling sensation. After this my fingers were caused to pass over the features of a face. I was thus able to assure myself that the face was not that of 'John.' Eusapia then pulled my hand sharply towards herself. A moment afterwards the same figure began to advance behind my back; at the same time the gleam from the doorway reappeared.

"Almost immediately Dr. Venzano announced that a hand had taken possession of his own, and was drawing it upwards. Soon afterwards we all heard the sound of a sonorous kiss above his head. And now the same very fine and long beard began to brush over the back of his hand, passing backwards and forwards. The impression felt by Dr. Venzano was sufficiently distinct to enable him to declare that this beard was shaped to a point. Then he was made to feel the hollow of a mouth, the upper jaw, the upper jaw of which had some teeth wanting on the right side.

"At this point Dr. Venzano remarked that these signs corresponded exactly with the characteristics of a very near relative, deceased."

To these details of M. Bozzano's report I must add some facts which are deeply impressed on my memory. When my hand, guided by another hand, and lifted upwards, met the materialised form, I had immediately the impression of touching a broad forehead, on the upper part of which was a quantity of rather long, thick, and very fine hair. Then, as my hand was gradually led downwards, it came into contact with a slightly aquiline nose, and, lower still, with moustaches and a chin with a peaked beard. From the chin the hand was then raised somewhat, until, coming in front of an open mouth, it was gently pushed forward, and my forefinger, still directed by the guiding hand, entered the cavity of the mouth, where it was caused to rub against the margin of an upper dental arch, which, towards the right extremity, was wanting in four molar teeth.

It should be mentioned that when my hand came in contact successively with the lock of hair on the forehead, the nose, and the chin with the pointed beard, the other which guided it pressed upon it and caused it to stop at each with manifest purpose, as though each of these represented a special sign. I must note also that on comparing the indications obtained with those typical of a person who was very dear to me, I did not remember whether the four molars were absent on the right or left side, and that later, after making special enquiries in the family, I was able to ascertain that this defect exactly corresponded with the conditions presented by the materialised form. This being premised, I will submit the case in question to a brief discussion.

In this case it is still less allowable to speak of hallucination than in the others. The materialised form, of which the profile was rendered visible to M. Bozzano, did not present itself in the same manner to the other sitters, who, however, were able to conjecture its presence on account of the disappearance of the gleam of light from the corridor, as soon as the materialised form came into such a position as to intercept it. The perfect coincidence between the tactile impressions received first by M. Bozzano, and afterwards by the writer, also contributes to prove the absurdity of any hypothesis of hallucination.

In contradistinction to the other cases described, we may observe in this one the absence of what may be called the *mise en scéne* which habitually recurs during mediumistic séances. In fact, the sitting developed a rich harvest of phenomena without the usual cabinet having been prepared, and without the presence of those objects which formed, as we have said, the paraphernalia of other séances. The only respects in which the usual practice of the experimenters was adhered to, were with regard to the harmoniousness of the group, and, without departing from the legitimate exigencies of control, the almost complete darkness of the surroundings. Thus in the present case darkness supplied the place of the cabinet, and materialisations were obtained instead of the usual telekinetic effects. It is only logical that this should so happen. The cabinet is, in fact, nothing but a more or less dark chamber which facilitates the condensation of the psycho-physical activities emanating from the medium, and the assemblage of instruments is only a means of preparation suitable for promoting the variety of the telekinetic manifestations. Now all these usual arrangements for a sitting, which are perfectly useless when it is desired to experiment in the dark, and with harmonious surroundings and sitters, may rather be considered as adjuncts to the causes and methods by which all mediumistic manifestations are held to be produced (Morselli). Apart from the aureole of mysticism with which many fanatics love to surround them, they are evidently merely the result of suggestion received from prolonged practical observation, which, though brought up again in America in 1847 by the classical and unexpected phenomena in the Fox family, has so ancient an origin that it may be met with in the form of ritual practised by all peoples and in all times (Vesme).

In the present case the problem of seeking for the will which directs the phenomenon is of much greater complexity. It must be remembered that in the execution of this manifestation two materialised forms took part. This fact becomes evident since, without the control of the medium being in any way relaxed, two large hands, which were not his own, seized M. Bozzano's head and forced him to turn towards the far end of the room, which was dimly lighted, where a second materialised form developed, having the appearance of the complete figure of a man. As for the materialised form which presented itself to my direct observation, offering the tokens typical of a deceased person who was dear to me, I can affirm that it was neither thought of nor expected by me. Moreover, as I at once declares when I did first think of it I certainly did not ask for proof of identity such as were afforded me. Then, too, among the tokens by which the materialisation revealed its identity it chose one which was only imperfectly known to me, and the accuracy of which I could only ascertan after making enquiries among my family. Nor could I have been influenced by an impression received from what had occurred just before to M. Bozzano. He had simply mentioned that his hand had been carried into contact with a human face, with a pointed beard, a fact which had been previously mentioned at sittings, and was insufficient to afford precise data for the identification of a face. Thus the possibility is excluded of direct suggestion conveyed to Mme. Paladino from myself or from the other sitters, to whom, as to the medium herself, the person who manifested himself to us was entirely unknown.

As to the medium, who remained during the whole séance in a state of profound trance, the only act of hers which might be suspected of being done with a purpose was that of raising M. Bozzano's hand to touch the human face, on which he recognised nothing characteristic except the pointed beard.

In the face of these conditions what conclusions can one deduce? In this case the dilemma referred to in relation to the previous case repeats itself. Either the phenomenon is produced under the direction of an intelligence foreign to the medium and to the experimenters, or the subconsciousness of Paladino succeeded in bringing forth from the innermost recesses of my thought, details known only by myself, and followed up this work of mind-reading by a liberation of physio-psychic energy which assumed the form and the character of two human beings, one of whom bore the typical traits of a deceased person with whom I was very familiar during his lifetime. And not only was the subconsciousness of the medium able to reveal facts which I could clearly remember but also circumstances which I had doubtless known of in the past, but which I had in large measure forgotten at the moment when the phenomenon occurred. I allude particularly to the number and position of the teeth found wanting at the extremity of the upper jaw of the mouth of the face, a point on which, as I afterwards found, the Intelligence regulating the manifestation was much better informed than I.

In the case of the medium Helene Smith, who was subjected to strictly scientific and careful examination by Prof. Fournoy, Mlle. Smith must have herself evoked the forgotten facts which existed latent in her cerebral centres (cryptomnesia) ; facts which emerged as soon as she was in a state of trance. In the case before us, on the contrary, the details concerning the molar teeth were not presumably reproduced by me, who was the almost unconscious depository of the knowledge, but by the medium herself, who was completely ignorant of the fact and who must have extracted it from the hidden mental recesses of my brain.

From what has been said it is easy to argue that if the supposition of the intervention of a will foreign to the medium and to the experimenters at the séance, is, at the present stage of our human knowledge and in the face of the possible acquisitions of science, an excessively daring one, the interpretation which we have set forth is not less daring: it is one which supposes an intricate concatenation of psychological relations and has no other value than that of remaining within the limits of probabilities least inacceptable to science in its present condition.

CASE VII.—This is briefly reported in M. Vassallo's little book: *Nel Mundo degli Invisibili*, and at greater length in M. Bozzano's volume, already quoted: *Ipotesi Spiritica e Teoriche Scientifiche*. The séance took place on the evening of December 20th, 1900, in the rooms of the Minerva Club. The group was formed of MM. Vassallo, Erba, Ramorino, Mme. Ramorino and myself. The control of Mme. Paladino was confided to me, on the right, and to Mme. Ramorino, seated on the left. The room was arranged as usual, and lighted, when the phenomenon occurred, by the candle in the ante-room. The narrative of this incident is taken from the special note which I made myself on the same evening, after the séance.

"In spite of the dimness of the light I could distinctly see Mme. Paladino and my fellow-sitters. Suddenly I perceived that behind me was a form, fairly tall, which was leaning its head on my left shoulder, and sobbing violently, so that those present could hear the sobs; it kissed me repeatedly. I clearly perceived the outlines of this face, which touched my own, and I felt the very fine and abundant hair in contact with my left cheek, so that I could be quite sure that it was a woman. The table then began to move, and by typtology gave the name of a close family connection who was known to no one present except myself. She had died some time before, and on account of incompatibility of temperament there had been serious disagreements with her. I was so far from expecting this typtological response that I at first thought that this was a case of coincidence of name ; but whilst I was mentally forming this reflection I felt a mouth, with warm breath, lunch my my ear and whisper, *in a low voice in Genoese dialect,* a succession of sentences, the murmur of which was audible to the sitters. These sentences were broken by bursts of weeping, and their gist was to repeatedly implore pardon for injuries done to me, with a fullness of detail connected with family affairs which could only be known to the person in question. The phenomenon seemed so real that I felt compelled to reply to the excuses offered me with expressions of affection, and to ask pardon in my turn if my resentment of the wrongs referred to had been excessive. But I had scarcely uttered the first syllables when two hands with exquisite delicacy applied themselves to my lips and prevented my continuing. The form then said to me : 'Thank you,' embraced me, kissed me, and disappeared."

I should state at this point that this extraordinary phenomenon did not for a moment rob me of calmness of observation, which was more than ever necessary under these circumstances, and that I did not cease to watch the medium, who was quite awake and visible to all, and remained notionless through the whole course of the phenomenon.

I will add also a detail of some importance for our conclusions. During the séance, in addition to the materialisation already described, Cavaliere Erba was placed in contact with the materialised form of a very robust man, the so-called spirit of "John" ; and Mme. Ramorino with the form of an old woman, who said she was one of her relatives and in fact had all the characteristics of one ; Prof. Porro with the form of a slight, delicate girl, who in a low voice said she was his daughter, Elsa, who died when scarcely seven years old, and finally M. Vassallo was embraced by the form of a youth, whose hands he held long in his own, and in whom he was convinced that he recognised his deceased son Naldino. With regard to these incidents, I refer the readers to the book by M. Vassallo, already quoted: *Nel Mondo degli Invisibili*.

One more observation. The medium, who was awake all through this séance, did not complain of fatigue of any kind at the end, and did not show any of the passing symptoms of discomfort generally observable after trance.

It is not possible, in relation to this incident, to suggest suspicion of hallucination or of fraud. The ensemble of my perceptions of contact as well as auditive ones (the latter shared by my fellow sitters), the typtological response in complete accordance with the perceptions themselves, and the fact that, in spite of the very dim light, Mme. Paladino was perfectly visible to me and to all those present, as well as her complete ignorance of the family details revealed, exclude absolutely both these hypotheses.

The most salient point in this case is in relation to the directing intelligence engaged in this phenomenon.

It is important to remember in this connection that the entity manifesting was unknown to the medium and to all the members of the group. Now the will that determined the phenomenon could certainly not be sought in me, because, at this moment, my thoughts were far from the subject, and, as I have already said, even if I had desired the materialisation of an entity representing someone I had known in life, the person who appeared is certainly not the one I should have willed and desired to see at that moment. This is so true that, when I learned the name by typtology, I thought that this was only a coincidence, until the apparition murmured in my ear the sentences which identified this person. Moreover, that my will was different from the will of the intelligence with which I was in communication is very clearly proved by the second part of the phenomenon. In fact, when I felt it my duty in reply to the phrases murmured in my ear expressing regret, excusing myself in my turn, and when I had already pronounced a few words, two hands were applied to my lips, in a truly delicate way, so as to prevent me from continuing.

Whence then came this will, so openly opposed to mine?

Can it be thought to have originated with Paladino, or with the experimenters? It is not worth while to consider the latter ; and as to the possible intervention of the active volition of the medium, we shall in that case be compelled to recognise in the subconsciousness of Eusapia faculties capable of extracting from the memory cells in my cerebral centres, without my will, and even contrary to my will, circumstances intimately connected with my family, which I should have preferred to be irrevocably forgotten. And, moreover, this subconsciousness, by virtue of the energies emerging from Eusapia, must have become concrete in an autonomous individual under the form and with the characteristics of a personality who had really lived ; must have become saturated with her moral conditions and must gave interpreted them with marvellous exactness by language, as appropriate in its dialect form as in its sentiment, overflowing with healthy morality.

So far concerning the incident which affects me in particular. But apart from this, we must remember that the subconsciousness of Mme. Paladino during the whole course of the séance was not limited to the personification of the entity who manifested to me ; but during the lapse of a little more than an hour, in the part of the séance preceding the incident which concerned me, as well as afterwards, it must have personified several other individuals, all endowed with special characters and all corresponding, with extraordinary tokens of identification, to the various entities which she claimed to represent. Such an interpretation, we do not hesitate to repeat, would be so extraordinary that we certainly cannot consider it less daring than the hypothesis of possible communication with the deceased.

In the séance from which we have extracted the incident in question, unlike the majority of the séances with Mme. Paladino, the manifestations followed one another whilst she was completely awake. This state of things, taking in account also the richness of the phenomena obtained, is doubtless due to the exceptionally harmonious condition the circle and to a special mediumistic condition on the part of the medium. This also proves (we have already noted this and shall see it still better in what follows in relation the question of the absence of light) that the state of trance may also be unnecessary for obtaining important phenomena whenever the mediumistic potentiality of the medium is intense and the harmony among the experimenters is complete. In this case, as a general rule, the exhaustion of the medium at the close of the séance is less, and we in fact observed that at the close of the séance in question she was in quite a normal condition, very different from that observed in her after a state of prolonged trance under discordant conditions. We have not used this term, discordant conditions, at hazard, because long experience has taught us that every time that elements in fundamental disagreement with each other are introduced into a séance, not only do the phenomena develop with greater effort and difficulty but movements occur on the part of Eusapia which suggest to those who attend a séance for the first time legitimate suspicion of fraud. All this is no doubt in direct ratio the discord occasioned by the lack of calmness and the suggestive attitude of those experimenters who, in the manifestations which are about to be produced, have set themselves to discover, at all costs, trickery on the part of Mme. Paladino.

It will be noted in this episode that the form of the woman, whose presence I recognised, materialised behind my shoulders, outside the cabinet. We see, in this case, that the room itself, on account of its being dimly lighted, performed the function of a cabinet.

I will not dwell upon the dialogue which I had with the materialised form, nor upon the words which were murmured in my ear in a low voice. In connection with this acoustic phenomenon I can only refer to what I have already written relative to the fourth case in this series.

CASE VIII.—This case, including a series of incidents of considerable interest, is taken from the report of a séance which in our opinion is the most important ever

The Study of Materialisations

held with Mme. Paladino as medium. This report was published in full in the *Revue d'Études Psychiques* in September, 1902 ; the late lamented L. A. Vassallo referred to it in a brave lecture given in Rome, during the same year, under the auspices of the Italian Press Association. The séance in question took place at Genoa, on the evening of May 1st, 1902, in the rooms of the Avellino family, on the third floor of No. 29, Via Caffaro. Those present at the séance were Prof. Morselli, M. and Mme. Louis Montaldo, M. Ernest Bozzano, M. and Mme. Avellino, their two sons, and myself, who was commissioned to draw up the report of the séance.

The dining-room had been selected for the séance ; it possessed one window only and we used the recess of this window for the cabinet. Several pieces of furniture were removed into the next room, and I myself was commissioned to prepare the cabinet. I covered the front of the window with a piece of dark red flannel, and to the ends of the curtains which were already there I fixed with pins two to bands of black cloth. The master of the house then kindly allowed me to choose a small iron bedstead, like a camp bed, which I placed inside the cabinet. I also chose a mattress and laid it upon the bedstead.

At a distance of about 8 inches from the cabinet a small rectangular table of white wood was placed.

A piano was standing diagonally across one corner of room on the right of the cabinet ; there were other pieces of furniture ranged against the walls, and several chairs. A photographic camera, mounted on a stand, provided M. Montaldo, occupied the opposite corner of the room the piano. ... The room was brightly lit by a lamp with an Auer gas burner, hanging from the centre of the ceiling.

Before the séance began Mme. Paladino was carefully searched. Some of her garments were taken off in our presence, and a more thorough and unrestricted examination was carried out by Mme. Avellino and Mme. Montaldo in an adjoining room, where the medium was completely undressed. It should be stated also that her clothes were examined by us one by one, and that we held them up to the light to assure ourselves that nothing was concealed.

The objects examined were: knickers knitted in red wool, white chemise, black cotton stockings, a petticoat corset-cover of pink flannel, a red flannel bodice and a woollen skirt. During the séances, let it be observed, Mme. Paladino never wears corsets. In the only pocket of her skirt we found a crumpled white handkerchief.

The medium put on her clothes again in the presence of the two ladies above mentioned, who never left her and brought her directly into the séance room.

The séance began at 10.30 p.m. During the first part, whilst the medium and the experimenters were sitting at the table forming a chain, many very interesting levitations of the table were witnessed. The incidents we are about to relate, however, took place during the second part of the séance. They are recorded as follows in a report which I dictated on the same evening, as soon as the experiments were over, and which was submitted for confirmation to all the sitters :

> "Almost at once, Eusapia arose, raised the curtains of the cabinet and lay down on the bed, to the bars of which Professor Morselli and M. Avellino bound her firmly. They fastened her wrists to the two iron bars on either side, by a cord with many knots ; they then passed the cord

twice round the waist of the medium, fastening the ends with many knots to the iron bars of the bed. Having carefully examined all the fastenings, Professor Morselli added a third, securing her feet by many knots to the cross bar at the foot of the bed.

"Then we all took our places on the two rows of chairs. In the first row were seated, in succession, ... M. Avellino, senior, myself, Professor Morselli, Mlle. Avellino, and M. Avellino, junior. In the second row, M. and Mme. Montaldo, Mme. Avellino, and M. Bozzano. The light was lowered, but so little that it was still possible to read—as Professor Morselli observed—the smallest type of a newspaper (nonpareil).

"After about fifteen minutes, the table, which was at a distance of a yard from us, and 8 inches from the cabinet, began to move itself. At first it rose on two feet, rapping several times. Soon afterwards the curtains moved as if they had been put aside by two hands and a large opening was made at the upper part, in which we could see the face of a young woman, the hand and the part of the body which was visible being enveloped in snowy white drapery. Her head seemed to be surrounded by many circular bands of this material, so that only a small oval portion of her face was seen, sufficient, however, to enable us to note with precision the eyes, the nose, the mouth, and the upper part of the chin. The apparition remained visible to all for nearly a minute. When M. Bozzano remarked that only a portion of the face was visible, the tips of two fingers were seen to draw aside the drape on either side, so as to show the contours more distinctly and completely. Before disappearing the figure bowed its head to salute us and sent us a kiss, the sound of which was perfectly audible to everyone.

"After a few minutes' interval the table began its automatic movements again. Then the curtains divided as if they had been opened from the inside by two hands, forming a large space in which the figure of a man presented itself, with a large head and strong shoulders ; he also was surrounded by white drapery, the head was covered in such a way that one could see through the light material the rosy tint of his face the nose standing in relief, also the eyebrows and the chin. M. Bozzano and Professor Morselli declare that they also observed a thick beard on the chin. This man's face remained visible for at least a minute. It bowed towards us several times and withdrew, having sent us several sonorous kisses accompanied by expressive movements of the head.

" When the curtains closed again the clapping of hands was heard inside the cabinet.

"At this moment we heard Eusapia's voice plaintively call Professor Morselli, who went into the cabinet and found her in same position in which he had fastened her. The medium in a state of trance, with evident signs of suffering, complained that her wrists were tied too tightly. Professor Morselli then set them free with much difficulty, on account of the complication of the knots ; Mme. Paladino then remained fastened only by her feet and waist.

"As Professor Morselli returned to resume his seat, M. Bozzano remarked that as the Professor was just under the lamp he was obliged, when looking towards the cabinet, to shade his eyes with his hand from the excessive light that fell from above; he therefore asked M. Avellino to kindly exchange places with the Professor. This was done; Professor Morselli then occupied the chair ..., and M. Avellino ... where Professor Morselli had previously sat.

"When all were in their places it was observed, almost at once, that the lid of the piano rose and fell automatically, producing a certain amount of noise. Almost at the same time we saw appear outside the curtain, on the right, the figure of a young woman, who was rather like the one I have described. The apparition bent her head repeatedly, bowing as if to salute us; then withdrew. On this occasion we were all impressed by a new fact of importance for readers who (*more solito*) are disposed to tell us that we were hallucinated. We observed that the figure in question, bending forward so as to remain at a certain distance from the wall, which was illuminated by the gas light, projected its shadow on the wall, and that this shadow followed all the motions of its body, which was evidently materialised.

"Meanwhile Professor Morselli, at the request of Eusapia, whose feeble and plaintive voice reached us from inside the cabinet, came with his chair close to the piano.

"A few moments later, another figure of a woman appeared on the same side of the cabinet at which we saw the preceding figure appear. Although this figure was in some respects like the other, there were some points of difference. The number of turns of the white bands twisted round the head was quite extraordinary; their outer edges projected in such a way that the face seemed buried in them. The trunk of the materialised body was surrounded by as large a number of folds; they looked like the swathings of an Egyptian mummy. The materialised form was so near to us that we were able to form a fairly correct conjecture as to the nature of the material. It seemed to us much thicker than ordinary gauze; but not so thick as batiste. The figure leant forward, resting its elbow on the top of the piano; we were then again able to notice a very curious fact. The fore-arm which we saw was evidently a stump, because the sleeve hung down over the front of the piano for at least a foot, right down to the lid of the keyboard. The apparition several times lifted and moved this half-formed limb, the shadow of which was thrown on the wall, and followed all its movements.

"The woman with the white bands had hardly returned to the cabinet when we heard fresh complaints from Mme. Paladino, who with renewed urgency begged Professor Morselli to liberate her from the fastenings, which pressed too tightly. The Professor hastened with the intention of freeing her from the two cords which still held her.

"*But to his great astonishment and ours, we found that the medium had been afresh tied at the wrists, and fastened to the two side bars of the bed by means of many turns of cord, which terminated in knots much more numerous and tighter than those which were made by Professor Morselli at the beginning of the sé-*

ance.

"This time Eusapia was untied not only at the wrists but also at the feet ; so that the fastening round the body was the only one which still held her to the bed.

"We had hardly taken our places again when the curtains opened at some height above the ground, and we saw in a large oval space the figure of a woman holding in her arms a little child, seeming almost as if she were rocking it. This woman, who looked about forty years of age, wore a white cap trimmed with white lace ; the cap, whilst hiding the hair, showed the features of a broad face with a high forehead. The remaining part of the body which was not hidden by the curtain was covered with white drapery. As to the child, as far as one could judge from the development of the head and body, it was about three years old. Its little head was uncovered, and had very short hair ; it was at a slightly higher level than that of the woman. The body of the child seemed to be enveloped in swaddling clothes, composed also of light and very white material. The woman was looking up affectionately at the child, whose head was slightly bent towards her.

"The apparition lasted more than a minute. We all stood up and approached it, so that we could perceive the slightest movements. Before the curtain closed again the woman's head was moved a little forward, whilst the child, bending several times to right and left, repeatedly kissed the face of the woman, so that the sound of the childish kiss reached our ears quite distinctly.

"During this episode Eusapia's complaints

continued and increased ; so that we decided to enter the cabinet. She was occupying the same position in which we had left her, and she seemed tired and suffering. Her breathing was difficult, her pulse very rapid and strong ; we were obliged to decide to close the séance. Mme. Paladino, still in trance, was freed from the last cord that bound her ; we made her get off the bed and she came and sat on a chair at one end of the table."

To the above report it will be advisable to add a few details, which on scrupulous scientific grounds I thought it better to omit, but which were noted by my companions, and in particular by M. Bozzano, who published them in his work already cited.

These details refer to the last episode and particularly to the woman who held in her arms a child, seemingly about 3 years old. Now, whilst we all clearly saw the cap trimmed with lace which completely hid the woman's hair, it was also observed that this cap terminated in two ends of rose-coloured ribbon which were tied under her chin ; this coloured ribbon was not noticed by myself (hence my silence about it) ; but I clearly remember having seen what looked like a rosy mark under the chin, a mark which I supposed belonged to the skin of the chin itself. I should also add that, from the position I occupied, I could only, unlike the others, get a very slanting view of the front of the right side of the neck of the materialised form.

Another peculiarity which I did not think necessary to mention in my report is the following, which I quote in full from M. Bozzano's account:

"The interest created in us by the whole wonderful picture which had become concrete in our presence, a real, living picture, expressing by spontaneous actions and movements of affection the tenderest sentiments of domestic life, was such that, as soon as the forms had retired behind the curtain, information was eagerly desired from the mediumistic personality of 'John.' The latter, through the mouth of the medium, replied: 'The woman's form was Mme. Avellino's mother ; the child she held in her arms was her grandchild, the child of Mme. Avellino.'"

Mme. Avellino, who was the only relative present who remembered her mother, who died while still young, could not, from the position she occupied, which, like mine, was sideways and behind the form that appeared, recognise the resemblance ; she remembered, however, one very interesting detail ; it was that her mother, in the last years of her life, had the habit of wearing a lace-trimmed cap, which, according to the fashion of the time, was fastened under the chin with rose-coloured ribbon. As to the child, she could not identify it, because she only saw the back of its head.

To be exact and complete in our record we should here mention that the photographic camera was frequently exposed by M. Montaldo, but that nothing except indefinite whitish blotches were obtained owing to the light being insufficient to impress the plates. On the last exposure, however, two distinct blotches were visible, which, by their position one in front of the other, we supposed might correspond to the forms of the woman and the child who appeared in the fifth manifestation.

In any case, on account of their indefiniteness, we did not think that any evidential value should be attached to the photographs obtained.

This terminates a series of incidents which, by reason of the conditions under which, and the manner in which, they were observed, provide data for interesting deductions.

With regard to the reality of the manifestations obtained, it would be useless to waste words. The phenomena were produced in light, in a place chosen by us and guarded by the strictest precautions, and the same precautions extended to the medium and her clothing.

A few words, however, may be said on the subject of one of the most salient phenomena of this case, that is to say, to the matter of the renewal of the knots at Paladino's wrist, which Prof. Morselli had untied a few minutes previously. We should consider whether it is possible that the medium could not have tied herself up again.

The phenomenon is so extraordinary that we have tried to consider all ways in which Eusapia might have tied it herself, and we have only been able to put forward a single theory, which, however, does not stand against the facts which have been stated.

The only supposition that can be suggested (although Eusapia was in a state of trance and was fastened to the bed by very strong bands round her waist and feet), is that she might with her free hands, by means of numerous loose turns of the cord, have succeeded in fastening them to the lateral bars of the bed, first on one side, then on the other, afterwards bringing the ends together in such a way as to be able to make a quantity of very tight knots, and then slipping her hands as far as the wrists into the space remaining between the turns of cord. But in this case the fastening that we had examined would have been found in a very different condition ;

that is to say, on account of the difference between the size of the hand, even when squeezed, and that of the wrist, we should not have found the latter adhering closely to the bars of the bed, fastened by such tight bonds around it that the marks were left on the skin. Neither would it have been necessary to use all the time and trouble taken by Prof. Morselli, aided by one of us (M. Avellino, junior) to liberate the hands from the cord.

The hypothesis which we have suggested is, therefore, not logically possible. If we thus exclude the hypothesis of fraud it is easy to see that that of an illusion of the senses cannot be entertained either. The duration of the apparitions, the perfect agreement of all the experimenters in observing them, the shadows they cast on the walls of the gas-lighted room, all serve to disprove every possibility of hallucination.

One of the most striking peculiarities of the materialisations observed, is that they appeared and remained visible for some time in such brilliant gaslight that it was possible, as Prof. Morselli observed, to read even the small print of a newspaper.

The objection is often raised that these mediumistic phenomena can only be produced in darkness. As we see, this example is an eloquent proof that the contrary is possible. The materialised forms which we saw resisted for some time the action of the light, and only required the obscurity of the cabinet in order to condense themselves before facing the light.

The reason for this power of resistance can only be found in the exceptionally favourable conditions of the sitters. We must recall in this connection a circumstance already mentioned by M. Bozzano with regard to the séance in question, namely, that two ladies, both of them gifted with considerable mediumistic power, were in the circle, and that they certainly contributed to reinforce the mediumistic powers of Eusapia.

We may consider it as proved by experience that everyone possesses a certain amount of mediumistic powers ; it has also been observed that there are some mediumistic faculties which, instead of being increased by combination, are weakened by it. It is evident that in this case the mediumistic faculties were homogeneous, the sum of them resulting in conditions which enabled the materialised forms to endure light for more than a minute.

In this case, in spite of the homogeneity of the circle and the high degree of intensity of the mediumistic power, we observed that the materialised forms clid not issue completely from the cabinet, and only showed a part of themselves. We even noticed that in the woman's form who leaned on the piano only the upper part of the arm and a portion of the forearm were fully formed. All this confirms what we have already said, that is to say, that with Eusapia, in contrast to what occurs with other mediums much more powerful than herself in this respect, it is very rare to obtain complete materialisations.

As in the preceding cases, before considering what may be the Intelligence which guided the phenomena, several facts should be made clear. In the first four apparitions we none of us recognised anyone we had known in life ; as to the two last, which appeared together, representing a woman and child, the faces could not be clearly seen ; it was only supposed, by the Avellino family and especially by Mme. Avellino, in consideration of the details we have mentioned, that these forms represented her mother and one of her children, who died at the age of about 3 years.

Some of us thought also that in the second form which appeared we recognised "Katie King," who appeared to Sir William Crookes through the mediumship of Florence Cook ; and in the third the form of "John," the so-called spirit-guide of Eusapia. We must observe that with these two materialisations no typtological information was given, and no word through the mouth of the medium confirmed the suppositions, which in the case of the so-called "Katie" were justified merely by a certain resemblance to the photograph taken by Sir William Crookes, a resemblance more obvious in the arrangement of the white draperies than in the face, and for the so-called "John King," the resemblance consisted in the vigorous aspect, the abundant beard, and the strong shoulders presented by the male form, characteristics which corresponded to the impressions produced generally by contact with this mediumistic personality.

4. Whence comes the will which directs the phenomena?

After these brief considerations we will consider in what direction the controlling will may rationally be sought for.

If we reflect on the first four incidents we shall be convinced that it could not emanate from any one of the experimenters. What occurred was absolutely novel and unexpected by them, and the forms which manifested offered no resemblance to persons whom, consciously or unconsciously, they might have desired to see.

The same cannot strictly be said of Eusapia, in spite of the fact that no typtological or verbal indications were made serving to identify the materialised forms. If we suppose that two of the apparitions were "Katie" and "John King," it would be possible to imagine that these materialisations were only the effect at a distance of the working of the medium's subconsciousness, a work engendered by association and by impressions received by the repetition of surrounding conditions and by frequent and prolonged suggestions on the 'part of experimenters ; in fact by an assemblage of circumstances, inherent in her mediumistic education, and therefore the result of a special determining cause.

As to the contemporaneous appearance of the woman and child, who were thought to represent the mother of Mme. Avellino and one of her sons who died whilst still very young, it is evident that the intelligence controlling this manifestation cannot be sought for in Mme. Avellino herself, and still less in the other sitters. As to the latter, in this case also the apparitions were both new and unexpected ; and the same applies to Mme. Avellino, who did not recognise the forms which appeared by any traits of physiognomy, and thought only that it might represent them on account of what Eusapia afterwards said and because of the cap trimmed with lace and tied with pink ribbon, a detail which is of considerable value as a token of identity.

The will directing the manifestation, considering the words uttered by Eusapia, might be traced to her. In this case, as in other preceding examples, we must suppose that her subconsciousness succeeded in extracting from Mme. Avellino's mnemonic centres certain peculiarities known by her alone and forgotten, and that it unconsciously translated them into action by means of a combination of energies rendered concrete at a distance and perceived by us as materialisations. We are obliged, in this instance also, to have recourse to a very complicated application of the biodynamic theory in order to explain these facts ; in a word, we are face to face with a fact which goes far beyond the limits of animistic phenomena. Up to this point these explanations might be allowed to pass, although they do not repose on any very solid basis. There is, however, one circumstance in the séance above described which in our opinion eludes even the most complicated explanatory conjecture : that is the incident of the re-tying of the knots at the medium's wrists, which had been untied by Dr. Morselli a short time before.

We have already shown that the hypothesis that Eusapia tied herself is not logically possible. By whom, then, we ask, was this long and camplicated manual work effected, and what brain directed this extraordinary phenomenon ?

Let us here recall three very important facts :

1st. That Prof. Morselli had liberated Eusapia's wrists only a short while before the third apparition was seen.

2nd. That the fresh fastenings were observed shortly after the appearance of the fourth apparition.

3rd. That between the third and fourth apparitions there was only a very brief interval of time.

This implies that a large proportion of the time which passed between the untying of the fastenings and the making of the new knots was occupied by the manifestations of the materialisations. Therefore, if the patient labour of tying the knots is to be reasonably attributed to any personality, we shall be obliged to admit the intervention of some other mediumistic personality, at work in the cabinet, contrary to the will of Eusapia, whose complaints and reiterated calls to Prof. Morselli afforded evidence of her sufferings.*

[* All these details certainly afford further proof of the reality of the materialisations obtained. If we make the absolutely inadmissible supposition that the medium, in spite of our control, artificially produced the observed manifestations, could she at the same time have made these detailed and complicated fastenings, which would alone require a considerable amount of time?]

We see then that for the execution of these manifestations a fresh personality and also a fresh will must have intervened, independent of our own, and in manifest opposition to the will of the medium ; a will, the genesis of which is unknown to us, and for which, as we do not wish to overstep the limits of admitted scientific possibility, we abandon the search.

In concluding these considerations we think it desirable to point out that, keeping always to the principle of psycho-dynamism, the properties of the subconscious show themselves to be not only extraordinary in relation to the production of living organisms, but also in the production of rich, luxuriant and varied kinds of fabrics which, as we have seen, adorned the materialised forms.

We were able during the incidents described not only to admire these fabrics close at hand, and to compare them with clothing habitually used, but also to observe the quantity (sometimes quite extraordinary) of the bands in which some of the materialised forms were enveloped ; we could also note how objects were reproduced fashioned according to the mode of past times, as for example a cap trimmed with lace and ending in two coloured ribbons, as several of us can testify.

Whatever theory be advanced the problem of materialisations is, as we see, a very difficult one, whether we desire to explain them by established laws, or to attribute them to *a conscious ego* independent of the medium, and which arranges the séance.

* * *

In the light of the facts related in this series of incidents the deductions arrived at on consideration of the preceding series acquire much greater importance. The phenomena this time assumed a much more elevated form, amounting to genuine apparitions of phantoms. We were able to assure ourselves that this was due to the fuller mediumistic capacity of Eusapia and to the homogeneity among the sitters. The importance of homogeneity in the circle, in relation to the suggestibility of the medium, makes it possible to suppose that many of the frauds which are attributed to her may be ascribed to suggestive thoughts of some of the experimenters who lack the necessary calmness of mind. We have observed that darkness is not always a necessary condition when the mediumistic power of Paladino is strong and the homogeneity of the circle complete.

In the greater number of the materialised forms perceived by us either by sight, contact, or hearing, we were able to recognise points of resemblance to deceased persons, generally our relatives, unknown to the medium and known only to those present who were concerned with the phenomenon.

In considering these extraordinary phenomena we have, each time, suggested a plausible interpretation in favour of those psycho-dynamic theories which are the boldest hypotheses which biology admits of. But we have not always found that these very complicated hypotheses fulfill all the exigences of the case, and sometimes we were obliged to recognise the intervention of an independent will which could not belong either to Mme. Paladino or to the experimenters.

We have not, however, considered it advisable to pass the confines of known natural laws in order to discover what this will may be ; we have preferred to maintain a strict reserve on this point, and this not from want of sincerity, but because we are mindful of the many lacunæ which exist in the domain of science ; with due respect, however, to the opinions of those savants who, although they began by denying all intelligence in these manifestations, afterwards became the adherents of an idealism which, independently of such experiments, has inspired many of the highest intelligences honoured by humanity.

5. Non-spiritistic Theory

At the beginning of this article we said, that out of many mediumistic phenomena of a physical kind which a long and uninterrupted series of experiments has enabled us to observe, we have cited only a few typical ones which were verified under conditions excluding all suspicion of fraud. In fact the conditions of light under which these phenomena were produced, the exceptionally rigorous precautions taken, the calmness in which the observations were made, with that degree of distrust and suspicion which should always accompany the observation of abnormal facts, the scientific sincerity of the experimenters, the common purpose of searching for truth without preconceptions — these conditions combine and supplement one another so as to give the manifestations obtained the most absolute imprint of genuineness.

We are thus dealing with incontestable phenomena, which are the more important because notable men familiar with mediumistic studies constantly deny the genuineness of physical manifestations. We have only to recall in this connection the campaign carried on by Dr.

Hodgson in the Proceedings of the Society for Psychical Research. Dr. Hodgson, assisted by Mr. Davey, who played the part of fraudulent medium in order to show the extent to which human witnesses can be duped, contrived and arranged a series of séances during which incidents occurred which those present considered to be real. It is enough to recognise that as soon as the truth was known the success of these séances made a great impression on many researchers and justified their suspicions ; so much so indeed that even Professor Hyslop recently expressed an unfavourable judgment as to the genuineness of physical phenomena. Now although the suspicion of these two experts, Dr. Hodgson and Professor Hyslop, is to some extent justifiable, it is the more noteworthy because as the result of patient and detailed study they had already come to the conclusion—based upon a large collection of intellectual phenomena — that it is necessary to assume the intervention of the spirits of the deceased.

In view of the incidents we have described, however, we affirm that our convictions are unshaken ; the errors into which others have fallen (and with which we are perfectly familiar) have only served as valuable instruction as to the conduct of our investigations ; we were constantly on our guard to avoid all possible distractions ; when the séance-room had been closed and sealed none of the experimenters left it for an instant. Moreover, the phenomena which we have cited occurred so spontaneously and under such conditions that several times we remember Professors Porro and Morselli, M. Vassallo and M. Barzini, whilst submitting Eusapia to the most severe control, recognised that this was superfluous, particularly in relation to the manifestations which occurred in full light, visible to all, beyond the reach of the medium and those who composed the circle. Finally, it should be borne in mind that Mr. Davey, in agreement with Dr. Hodgson, utilised for the accomplishment of his tricks the moments in which he had succeeded in distracting the attention of the enquirers ; whereas in the séances with Eusapia, the investigators were almost always warned when phenomena were about to occur, either by verbal communication from the medium, or by typtology, or by some other characteristic sign, which, instead of distracting, served to increase the attention of the sitters.

Mediumistic manifestations, whether of the simplest parakinetic or telekinetic phenomena, or the much more complex one of materialisation, do not, in our opinion, bear that character of triviality which even many eminent investigators have attributed to them. Although at times they may appear grotesque, even when considered merely as physical phenomena and independently of the intellectual note which always accompanies them, they are of great value, and are worthy of attention and study, because they indicate the existence of unknown laws and open the way to fresh scientific discoveries. The physical phenomena of mediumship cannot be and ought not to be considered trivial, any more than the spasmodic movements of the limbs of a decapitated frog, which resulted in the discovery of the Voltaic pile.

We should add to these considerations the fact that intention is constantly manifested in these phenomena. Whether they actually obey a controlling intelligence, whose origin is in the medium, or which proceeds from the sitters and operates through the medium, or whether there is an independent controlling intelligence, foreign to both, the origin of which cannot at present be found, in any case it is a fact of enormous magnitude to recognise that, under the influence of will, energy is exteriorised which results in effecting the simplest and also the most complex phenomena of mediumship.

We have seen that in order to give a possible explanation of the phenomena of materialisation it was necessary to have recourse to the psycho-dynamic theory, as being, of the theories accepted by Science, the one which seems most probable.

With regard to the intellectual phenomena, in the majority of cases, it has been thought necessary to seek their origin in the peculiar qualities of the subconsciousness of the medium.

In this connection we have not thought it necessary to consider the theory of psychic dissociation of personality which Dr. Pierre Janet constructed upon the masterly observations made by him upon various subjects in a state of hypnotic somnabulism.

Such a theory is in no way applicable to our case, for the following reasons. Dissociations of personality, as Dr. Janet has shown, can give rise to real individualisations, but these resulting personalities are only secondary ones, with limited intellectual faculties. Moreover, they are only portions of a disrupted consciousness, so that the greater the dissociation, the less is the psychic activity of the normal consciousness. The proof of what we have just said is the fact that, when the dissociated faculties are capable of composing a complete subconscious personality, endowed with a certain amount of independence, the normal personality is so impoverished that it cannot subsist as an entity, and the subject falls into a deep sleep, thus permitting the sub-hypnotic personality to emerge.

Nothing of this sort, as we see, is to be met with in the phenomena we have described. The personalities who manifest not only appear as materialised forms, visible and tangible, but are gifted with intellectual faculties which are the reverse of small, and which reflect the feelings and affections of the individuals which they claim to represent, calling up with wonderful correctness circumstances and details of facts unknown to the medium, known to few of us, and sometimes even long forgotten.

Moreover, these personalities, though they often reveal themselves whilst Eusapia is in trance, appear also when she is perfectly awake, in full mental self-possession, in such a way as to take keen interest in the phenomena which are being developed through her mediumship. Consequently the hypothesis of possible mental dissociation cannot be advanced with regard to the phenomena which we have described, and we have thought it unnecessary to refer to it when discussing them.

No theory, therefore, is at present more available as a tentative interpretation of a very large number of mediumistic phenomena than the biodynamic theory. We say "of a very large number," because we have shown that, in the case of many of the incidents set forth, the biodynamic theory appears insufficient as an interpretation. All mediumistic phenomena of a purposeful kind must start from some directing intelligence and will. This may originate in the medium direct, or indirectly by suggestion, conscious or unconscious, from those present at the séance. In many cases, however, the origin of this will seems to me to be quite independent of either medium or sitters. We have observed phenomena in which the directing intelligence was absolutely independent of the influence of the sitters and. was not only independent of the medium but in manifest opposition to her. These contrary personalities, so to speak, are frequently noticeable in experiments with Eusapia. Often, when she was awake, tired, and suffering from too great protraction of the séance, we noticed that she urged that it should be closed, whilst on the other hand the personality calling himself John insisted quite with paternal determination that the séance should continue.

"It must not be supposed," M. Bozzano has well said, "that these are instances of contrary personalities, such as appertain to many psycho-pathological subjects who, during the hallucinatory trance, are often in constant struggle with individualities which are merely the product of their diseased brains. The personalities described by us, with which the will of the medium is in conflict, are not the product of hallucinated brains ; they are actual personifications, which can be rendered objective, either to sight, or contact, or hearing ; they are real creations having the aspect of a human form."

The existence therefore of an independent will, the genesis of which cannot be found either in the medium or in the sitters, whatever skeptics may say, is a fact that our long and calm experiments have led us to consider as beyond all doubt, and which causes our opinion (with all due deference to the illustrious savant) to be contrary to that of Prof. Morselli, who holds that the medium thinks intensely of the phenomena and wills them, and it is also contrary to the opinion recently expressed by Prof. Grasset, who, whilst he entirely denies the genuineness of the greater number of the phenomena which official science has to a large extent accepted, believes that the ideas expressed by mediums during the state of trance only reflect the content of their own mental centres.

With regard to the assertion of Prof. Morselli, we accept it as true in a great many cases, and as evidenced to some extent by the synchronism between the movements of the medium and the development of the phenomena. We regard his assertion, however, as too absolute when he applies it to all the physical phenomena of mediumship.

It seems to us inadvisable to pause to discuss here the opinions of Prof. Grasset. The distinguished professor of Montpellier is too deeply rooted in his systematic negation of the facts of mediumship to express an impartial and calm judgment with regard to them. Moreover, besides showing that he has had very little personal experience, his writings are as full of quotations which seem to support his theories, as they are reserved and unfair in estimating the results arrived at by those experimenters whose conclusions differ from his own.

6. The Spiritistic Theory

We have already stated the reasons why, in our search for the will of which we could not discover the source in medium or experimenters, we have been careful not to accept *ipso facto* theories which pass beyond natural laws. The region of the unknown is too vast, and its possibilities are too numerous, to allow the human intellect for the present, at least, to advance further into the domain of metaphysical speculations. We must, however, recognise that if we were not allowed to contemplate the possibility of new scientific discoveries, we should be compelled to admit without reserve the real intervention of a spiritual entity foreign to living human beings ; we should be forced, in a word, to accept in full the spirit hypothesis.

At this point we may ask the question : Does this theory rest on so insecure a basis that we are bound to consider it absurd and untenable ?

The Study of Materialisations

We must first say that when we speak of the spirit hypothesis we mean only that which is founded upon the experimental demonstration of the survival of the soul as based on the study of facts which tend to prove the possibility of communicating with the deceased, while discarding all the dogmatic doctrines with which many adherents have surrounded it ; doctrines which have been derived from communications by writing or typtology, sometimes lofty in tone, but often contradictory, and too readily accepted as being messages from beyond the grave.

Thus regarded, we are convinced that the spirit hypothesis has the right to take its place with others as a living theory.

In the first place, apart from the evidence afforded by mediumistic phenomena as to the survival of the soul, the conception is not in itself an absurd one. In fact if we admit (what there is no reason for denying) the dualism of living beings, that they are composed of mind and matter, it is not absurd to suppose, not only that the mind may survive the body, but that a discarnate mind (as we say) may be able to communicate with the living.

When we turn to mental mediumistic manifestations we find that experts like Mr. Myers, Dr. Hodgson and Prof. Hyslop (without citing others), after prolonged experiments, rigorously carried out, collected and discussed, have become convinced of the possibility of actually communicating with the souls of the deceased. This is a very impressive circumstance, which has just drawn from Prof. Morselli (in spite of his aversion to the spirit hypothesis) the important sentence: "As a student and a philosopher I remain indifferent or shrug my shoulders when it is objected that Sardou is, or Gladstone was, a spiritist ; but I cannot assume this attitude when I see that an A. R. Wallace and a Barrett are spiritists, or that a Brofferio has become one through Eusapia, and a Hyslop through Mrs. Piper."

Neither do the physical phenomena of spiritism justify this assumed absurdity of the spiritistic theory. Sir William Crookes has not made any pronouncement as to the possibility of communication with the deceased, but thanks to the wonderful séances held with Home and Florence Cook, he has felt himself able to affirm the intervention of real spirit individualities extraneous to himself and to those present with him.

With regard to Eusapia's phenomena we can only refer to the conclusions we have drawn from them, recalling the fact that, if we were not obliged to take account of the numerous lacunæ in scientific knowledge, many of the incidents related, so far from necessitating prudent reserve, would have decided us in favour of the existence of spirit entities.

It is therefore obvious, in view of the physical manifestations obtained, that the spirit hypothesis seems to us far from being absurd. In fact, the only substantial difference between the biodynamic theory and the spiritistic theory consists in the origin of the intelligence which directs the manifestation ; the first theory ascribes the phenomena to the medium, the second attributes them to independent entities belonging to the spirit world. In both cases, however, the phenomena are produced by means of faculties peculiar to the medium with the probable assistance of the psychic forces of the investigators, under the operation of laws largely unknown and under conditions which determine the nature of the manifestation.

As we see, the science of biology is in no way contradicted by the spirit theory, and there is full justification for the ideas which we expressed at the outset of this article, which may be summed up in the words of John Stuart Mill: " Positivism does not deny the supernatural : it is content to relegate it to the origin of all things. Science contains nothing repugnant to the hypothesis that every event is the result of the specific will of a sovereign power, provided that this will adheres in its particular volitions to the general laws which it has itself imposed."

There are yet a few more considerations of a philosophical nature that we think it necessary to mention because they are derived from this same psycho-dynamic theory, which we have preferred to employ in attempting to interpret the phenomena occurring with Paladino.

"Among the reasons which suggest that one of the causes of the world may be an Intelligence," writes Brofferio, "is the fact of evolution ; evolution is not comprehensible apart from the finality of nature." The world in its invariable manifestations proceeds gradually and necessarily towards perfection, and in its slow and progressive work of natural selection we see the perpetual triumph of the most evolved, and the inexorable condemnation of that which does not correspond to a purpose. Now the psycho-dynamic theory, when applied to metapsychical mental manifestations as well as to the physical ones, would lead us to suppose that there exist in the sub-consciousness of the living organism peculiar, extraordinary and marvellous properties enormously surpassing those of the normal consciousness.

In relation then to that principle of finality above referred to, is it possible rationally to admit that these faculties exist latent in the depths of the subliminal consciousness, without any object, and are simply destined to perish with the cessation of life? Or, are we not rather driven by logical necessity to the conclusion that, instead of coming to an end with the body, they survive as indestructible faculties of the spirit, which tends ceaselessly towards a higher destiny?

Certainly no one would wish to ignore the force of these arguments in favour of the survival of the soul, arguments which have been already discussed at length by M. Bozzano, with his usual ability, in three articles. We may recall also, in this connection, the able writings of that eminent philosopher, Carl du Prel, who believed that the human soul resided in the subconsciousness.

If the genuineness of mediumistic phenomena has been to a large extent accepted by many eminent representatives of official science, this is due—and it should be confessed without reserve or innuendo—to spiritists. I myself have valued friends among them with whom I shared not only the search for truth, but also painful hours of struggle, of scorn and sarcasm, at a time, not far distant, when even to speak of mediumship was enough to make anyone laugh. It is due to them, and to their constant and persistent activity, that this difficult subject, so misconceived by prejudiced minds, was taken up by famous savants, who, when they have examined and certified the facts, have, most of them, acknowledged their indisputable genuineness.

We have thought it only just to recall, as Prof. Richet has already done with calm impartiality, the merits attaching to men who in difficult times, with earnestness and tenacity, in spite of fierce opposition, drew the attention of scientific men to a much despised order of phenomena.

At the same time we recognise that the diligent and uninterrupted labour of spiritists would certainly have done more to prepare the way for subsequent investigators if they had not been in such a hurry to raise a scaffolding of unverifiable theories, which they have prematurely tried to exalt to the rank, of a religious creed.

In saying this we do not wish to undervalue the importance of what spiritists have done, by keeping in view an object of the highest moral importance ; we cannot even deny that in time, and with the assistance of a more solid and secure basis of facts, their object may be obtained.

The spiritists are therefore true pioneers in that branch of science which includes the study of mediumship, and it is sincerely to be hoped that history may not reserve for them the fate of enquirers into magnetism, whose eminent names were gradually forgotten when, principally under the auspices of Charcot, the experiments of Mesmer were systematised according to criteria more conformable with modern science, and were appropriated by the latter under the name of " hypnotism."

* * *

The subject of mediumship is, we are told, vast and almost unexplored. And this is not surprising when we remember that the rediscovery of mediumistic phenomena took place towards the middle of the last century (the neospiritualism of Prof. Morselli), and that if the disciples of spiritism were numerous, there were very few who studied these phenomena in a strictly scientific manner. Recently, the study of these phenomena has been taken up with keen interest, particularly by persons who formerly considered it an indication of weak intelligence and a tendency to mysticism.

This, we confess, has given us such deep satisfaction that it has to a considerable extent compensated us for the bitterness which was formerly our lot. Having for many years past been convinced of the reality of the supernormal manifestations which we have ourselves observed under various circumstances with different subjects and under strict conditions, we have never for a moment withdrawn from the struggle, endeavouring above all to bring into the field of research the most eminent representatives of science, being assured that their acceptance of the reality of metapsychical phenomena would soon increase the number of researchers, and that our labours would be seconded by courageous co-operators. We were also persuaded that mediumistic phenomena being matters for observation, and not for experiment, as M. Camille Flammarion has justly pointed out, everyone can contribute his observations of facts. We should not possess, indeed, that rich and classic collection of instances of telepathy to be found in *Phantasms of the Living* if persons of various social classes had not seen and observed, and if experts like Gurney, Podmore and Myers had not enquired into and collected their observations.

Careful observation, made under conditions suitable for affording evidence of the reality of mediumistic phenomena, may be within the reach of anyone. But there is nothing more reprehensible than unwholesome dilettantism resulting from mere curiosity, which is responsible for much prejudice, particularly if the observers are excitable. It is for this reason that it is specially incumbent upon men of science to undertake this difficult research, men whose extended culture has enabled them to acquire the calmness necessary for forming a just estimate and opinion. To them, and more particularly to psychologists who cultivate that branch of knowledge which assists more than any other in the solution of these difficult problems, belongs this perplexing duty.

Nevertheless we differ entirely from Professor Morselli when he asserts that the right of passing decisive judgment exclusively appertains to psychologists and specially to those who hold academical degrees in that science. We agree with him that the solution of this arduous problem will be found in psychology, but we cannot follow him when he reserves the right to express valuable opinions exclusively to those who can exhibit a University diploma. In this the facts fully justify us. If we consider the most important works on the psychology of mediumship, we find names such as Robert Hare, Sir Oliver Lodge, W. F. Barrett, Ermacora, Crookes, who are, or were, eminent physicists ; Du Prel, philosopher and physician ; Zöllner, astronomer ; Hodgson and Myers, philosophers and men of letters ; Mrs. Verrall, professor of classical languages ; Gurney, Aksakoff, Podmore, without academical titles. Sidgwick, William James, and Hyslop are almost the only names among professors of psychology.

In closing this article, we wish to state that we make no pretension of setting forth anything new, and still less of arriving at absolute deductions. Our chief aim has been to set forth facts tending to prove the reality of the physical phenomena of mediumship, so much debated, whilst in so doing confining ourselves to the most rigorous rules of scientific precision, and conforming our deductions to the laws dictated by logic.

We know that eminent authors are now preparing to present the public with the results of their researches. Let them do so. We await their publications with a calm mind but with real interest, being ready to modify our ideas if the arguments of others succeed in convincing us, and ready also, within the limits of our knowledge, to discuss them if they do not express our convictions. We are not influenced by preconceived opinions of any kind ; our constant motto is the old maxim : *Amicus Plato, amicus Cicero, sed magis amica veritas.* Our chief desire, however, is that these important scientific investigations should be pursued with assiduity and perseverance, with the object of carrying conviction to those who are still tormented with doubts as to the reality of these phenomena, and that by an increase in the number of researchers the clash of various opinions may lead to the discovery of truth. There are no discussions more fruitful than those which serve to dissipate the darkness which shrouds the unknown. Let us hope that these discussions may be always conducted in a spirit of loyalty, with mutual respect and mutual tolerance.

On The Threshold of the Unseen:
Eusapia Paladino
(1917)

By Sir William F. Barrett, F.R.S

AFTER the favourable reports by Professor Charles Richet and Sir Oliver Lodge upon their experiments with Eusapia, further séances were held with her at Cambridge in 1895. I was not present, and, indeed, have never had the opportunity nor the desire to *experiment* with Eusapia, but those present at Cambridge came to the conclusion, on what appeared to them to be an adequate trial, that there was clear evidence of trickery on the part of Eusapia, although Sir Oliver Lodge adhered to his opinion that the phenomena he witnessed in the Ile Roubaud were genuine. This opinion was corroborated by that of the eminent physiologist, Professor Charles Richet. After the séances at Cambridge he for a time suspended his judgment, but subsequently, both in conversation with myself and on other occasions, has stated that he was absolutely convinced of the supernormal character of some of the manifestations which occur with Eusapia. This also was the opinion of the well-known astronomical writer, Camille Flammarion, who in his work, "Les Forces Naturelles Inconnues," deals at length with the phenomena occurring with Eusapia, and is convinced of their supernormal character.

But the most remarkable testimony in favour of Eusapia came from some of the leading scientific men of

Italy, men specially trained in the investigation of psychological and physiological phenomena. Perhaps the most notable witness was the late Professor Lombroso, who conducted the investigation of Eusapia's powers in his laboratory in the University of Turin, every precaution being taken against fraud. The result was that Lombroso publicly bore witness to the genuineness of these extraordinary physical manifestations. The opinion of so experienced and able a criminologist as Lombroso—wbose high scientific status is recognised throughout Europe—necessarily carried great weight. In an article published in 1908 in the "Annals of Psychical Science," Lombroso refers to various phases of these phenomena, including phantasms and apparitions of deceased persons. He points out that sometimes several phenomena occurred simultaneously, and hence were beyond the power of one person to perform, and also that there is evidence of the intrusion of another will, which could not be attributed to the medium or to any person present, but which was in opposition to all, and even to the control, "John." He lays stress upon the importance of these facts in relation to the hypothesis that the occurrences are explicable by the "psychic forces" of the medium and circle alone: an hypothesis which at an earlier stage of the inquiry he himself adopted, but which he now regards as inadequate. Independent testimony came from Dr. Enrico Morselli, Professor of Neurology and Psychiatry (mental therapeutics), in the University of Genoa, who presided over a set of séances with Eusapia in that city.

The control of the medium was very strict. Her hands and feet were held by Dr. Morselli and Sig. Barzini, editor of the "Corriere della Sera," who states that he was present "with the object of unmasking fraud and trickery," but was in the end convinced of the reality of some of the phenomena. The person of the medium was thoroughly searched before the séance, and the room was also searched; the light was never entirely extinguished.

Under these conditions Dr. Morselli testifies to the occurrence of the following phenomena: movements of the table, raps on the table and sounds on musical instruments without contact; complete levitations of the table; movements of objects at a distance from the medium seen in the light, and, also, the operation of self-registering instruments by the unseen agency; apports, i.e., objects brought into the room from outside; the sound of human voices not proceeding from any visible person; impressions on plastic substances of hands, feet, and faces; the appearance of dark prolongations of the medium's body, of well delineated forms of faces, heads and busts. Although entirely skeptical at the outset of his experiments, he declares himself convinced that most of the phenomena alleged to occur with Eusapia are "real, authentic, and genuine."

Dr. Morselli was disposed to interpret these phenomena by what he terms the hypothesis of special *psychic or bio-dynamic forces*; that is to say, he attributes them to some peculiar power emanating from the person of the medium. This is practically the psychic force theory of many earlier English investigators.

Shortly after the séances held under the direction of Dr. Morselli in the University of Genoa, another series of experiments in Turin, was conducted by Doctors Herlitzka, C. Foà, and Aggazzotti; Dr. Pio Foà, Professor of Pathological Anatomy, being present at the most remarkable of this set of experiments. These séances yielded similar positive results to those held by Professors Lombroso and Morselli.

Another competent witness is Dr. Giuseppe Venzano, stated by Dr. Morselli to be an "excellent observer." He contributed an important article to the "Annals of Psychical Science" (August and September, 1907), containing a detailed record and critical analysis of his experiences with Eusapia. under conditions of strict control, and sometimes in the full light given by an electric lamp of sixteen-candle power. Dr. Venzano, in the course of his experiments with Eusapia, the light in the room being sufficient to enable both the medium and his fellow-sitters to be clearly seen, perceived a woman's form beside him, felt her touch and heard her speak: the form spoke with fulness of detail of certain family affairs not known to anyone present except himself. The whole incident is a most amazing one, and Dr. Venzano states that, in his opinion, any explanation of this experience based on the possibility of fraud or of hallucination is impossible.

Professor Philippe Bottazzi, Director of the Physiological Institute at the University of Naples, having read the report of Dr. Morselli's experiments at Genoa, made an attempt to verify the phenoniena by means of an elaborate and carefully arranged set of sell-registering instruments, in the hope of obtaining an automatic graphic record of the psychic force exercised by the medium. Such a record would negative the hypothesis of hallucination or misdescription on the part of the oberver. These important experiments, carried out with the collaboration of several able professors of the same University, were remarkably successful, and Professor Bottazzi's article concludes by stating that these experiments have "eliminated the slightest trace of suspicion or uncertainty relative to the genuineness of the phenomena. We obtained the same kind of assura nce as that which we have concerning physical, chemical, or physiological phenomena. From henceforth skeptics can only deny the facts by accusing us of fraud and charlatanism."

In 1909 three members of the S.P.R., the Hon. Everard Feilding, Mr. W. W, Baggally, and Mr. Hereward Carrington were commissioned by the Society to carry out another serious investigation with this medium. The selection was specially made with a view to the qualifications of the investigators. Mr. Carrington was a clever amateur conjuror, and for ten years had carried on investigations on these physical phenomena in the United States. His book on this subject shows his familiarity with the methods adopted by fraudulent mediums and his cautious attitude towards all such experiences. Mr. Baggally was also an amateur conjuror with much experience, and had come to a negative conclusion as to the possibility of any genuine physical phenomena. Mr. Feilding's attitude was the same, and, moreover, he had had extensive experience in investigating physical phenomena.

The result of this investigation was that all three of these well-qualified men were convinced of the absolute genuineness of the remarkable supernormal phenomena they witnessed at their hotel in Naples.

Since then they have had another series of séances which yielded quite different results and in which they obtained nothing convincingly supernormal and much that was obviously normal and probably spurious. The same thing was also found in sittings with Eusapia in America. How can we reconcile these conflicting results? I am not concerned to defend Eusapia; on the contrary I am more disposed to loathe her, but we must be fair, and give even the devil his due. Like other psychics, especially those who exhibit similar amazing supernormal phenomena, she is most sensitive to "suggestion," even when unexpressed ; and in the trance, when her consciousness and self-control are largely inhibited, she is the easy prey of external influences ; in the absence of the steadying, though subconscious, influence of a high moral nature, she unblushingly cheats whenever the conditions are unfavourable for the production of supernormal phenomena. We have no right to assume that she is wholly cuscious of so doing, for Professor Hyslop has shown that mediutnship is often accompanied with abnormal bodily as well as mental conditions. We know little or nothing of what constitutes the peculiar faculty or environment for the necessary production of these physical phenomena. If they are due, as some have thought, to an externalization of the nerve force of the psychic, it is not improbable that the degree of this externalization will vary with the favorable or unfavorable mental state of those present. We may even conceive that when this psychic force is restricted or not externalized, it may create movements of the limbs of the psychic which will cause her to perform by normal actions (in perhaps a semiconscious state) what under good psychical conditions would be done supernornially. This would produce the impression of intentional fraud. Everyone who has had much experience in these perplexing investigations knows that what seems purposeless and stupid fraud often intrudes itself, after the most conclusive evidence of genuine phenomena has been obtained. It is this which renders the whole enquiry wholly unfitted for the hasty and unskilled investigator.

Psychical and Supernormal Phenomena: Experiments Made With Eusapia Paladino at Genoa by Professor Morselli

By Dr. Paul Joire

We shall in this chapter consider the very complete study made on the phenomena produced through Eusapia Paladino at Genoa by Professor Morselli.

Eusapia Paladino is mainly a physical medium; and if students of psychical matters have preferred to go to her, it is because she has consented to hold sittings under the control of men of science, and has accepted, up to certain limits imposed by the form of her mediuniship, unusual conditions of experiment; she has also submitted to examination which no medium had ever previously permitted. In this respect Eusapia's attitude is worthy of praise, and her position as a medium ought to be regarded with less distrust.

Intellectual mediumship, which takes place through subjective psychological processes in the medium, is not susceptible of scientific investigation except by consummate psychologists; and of those there are, in truth, not too many, and moreover psychology, although dabbled in by fashionable dilettantism, is not a study within the reach of all. Physical mediumship, on the other hand, is manifested in objective, tangible, visible facts, which can therefore be perceived by the senses of the sitters, and ascertained and, up to a certain point, measured by mechanical means and apparatus. Physical mediumship, therefore, comes within the scope of experimental research, under which name we include also the simple observation of phenomena as they occur naturally and spontaneously, and the analysis of their causes.

There can no longer be any doubt as to the reality of Eusapia's phenomena. They have now been seen by too many persons under excellent conditions of verification, with the full certainty that the medium had not her hands and feet free, and that many of the phenomena occurred at a distance which excluded all possibility of deception ; and there are now too many trustworthy men, accustomed to observe and experiment, who say that they have become convinced that Eusapia's mediumship is genuine. We have now got far beyond the time when her phenomena could be explained by the exchange of hands and feet in the dark ; the method of inquiry into her phenomena is very different, and so is her attitude in the sittings, especially when she is watched by persons not bound by preconceptions and by fear of trickery, and in whom she has confidence. In fact, none of the most celebrated mediums are accredited by so many explicit declarations by scientific men of the foremost rank ; no one, from Home and F. Cook onward, has allowed the introduction into the sittings of scientific instruments and methods with so much tolerance as Paladino.

The general public, on reading the accounts of the sittings, cannot always form a precise and complete conception of the conditions under which the phenomena are witnessed. Each phenomenon would require such minute particulars to every element of fact as to the position and gestures of the medium, the chain formed by the observers, the psychic state of each of them, the control for verification, the development, duration, and intensity of the manifestations, the preparations and consecutive circumstances, &c., that the description would become perfectly unreadable, and impossible to grasp as a complete mental picture. Luigi Barzini has done admirably, but not all of Eusapia's sittings can hope to have such an able and readable chronicler.

It follows that the public distrusts the accounts, or is not convinced by them ; and many skeptics, every time that phenomena are related, recommence their usual eternal questionings, dictated by doubt. Everything is an occasion for incredulity to those who obstinately remain, or pose as, skeptics: the control of the hands, the position of the feet, the attitude of the head, the distance of the object, the attention of the two watchers to right and left, the convulsions of the medium, the emotions of the spectators, the degree of light. This last point especially arrests the doubters ; we feel them always turning to the question of darkness, as though the séances were always held in the dark, and as though students, especially after long practice, were incapable of making use of their senses and of their perceptive centres, simply because there was no light!

It is useless to reply exhaustively to such objectors ; they return to the charge and repeat their remarks as though they had made new discoveries, and as though they alone, the incredulous who have not seen, possessed the key of the secret.

Many *say*: "I will believe when I see it." While this is all well and good, meanwhile they believe, without verification, that Nansen reached 86° 4" north latitude, but not that I have been present at a real levitation of a table or at a visible or tangible materialisation of a hand.

They are within their rights, but Eusapia cannot be at everyone's service, and her mediumistic phenomena can not serve as a theatrical show.

Some put forward a condition for their belief; they appeal to the criterion of authority, and say that they *will* believe when such and such a man of science, "the man, who is above all suspicion," shall have made certain of the matter. Well, while I was and declared myself a skeptic in regard to spiritism and psychism, people did me the honour to point me out as a judge to whom appeal might be made, and this was said and printed in 1892. When, however, I admitted that I had seen and touched the reality of mediumistic facts at the Minerva Club, I lost my position with doubters as an "authority above suspicion," and in 1902 a brilliant journalist, engaged in a superficial anti-spiritistic campaign, dethroned me from this position, though not much to my regret, and invoked the superior authority, &c., &c., of Professor Blaserna of Rome.

I am convinced that Blaserna, if he had been present, as I was, at about thirty sittings with Eusapia (not at one or two only, which are not enough for a serious judgment, would have seen, touched, and perceived with his senses that which I have seen, touched, and perceived with mine, and that even he, the distinguished secretary of the *Academia dei Lincei*, would end by losing the confidence of the obstinate doubters.

Neither I nor Blaserna, nor any one else, can change the substance of facts, when hundreds of persons endowed with senses and brains, not different from our own in morphology and function, assert and confirm each other in the assertion that they have not been the victims either of deceptions or of illusions. It is time that there was an end of this negationist attitude *á outrance*, of this habit of constantly casting the shadow of doubt and directing the smile of sarcasm, I will not say upon the moral respectability (for in science all are subject to caution), but upon the common sense of the observers who make assertions.

Eusapia, like other individuals endowed with her metapsychical powers, would certainly have taken another empirical direction, if, as was the case with Stainton Moses and Mme. d'Esperance, she had been left to herself (I ought to say, however, that she is completely lacking in initiative). But she was discovered and developed between 1872 and 1882 by Signor Damiani, an ardent spiritist, who, on his return from England, where he had learned the American technique of spiritism, introduced it into Naples and rendered it automatic in Eusapia. M. Chiaia, who succeeded Damiani, simply followed in the same track.

It is true that, given the nature of the experiments, there is nothing much better to be done ; but, at all events, it might be said that the spiritists fear to detach themselves from their antiquated and crude paraphernalia. Eusapia is therefore automatically bound to this "technique" and cannot free herself from it ; but this is not to be charged entirely against her. It is the whole history of spiritism that is summed up in her, and she is not to blame.

On the other hand, there seems to be some reason for the habitual technique of spiritism. Take, for example, the darkness or the feeble light or the red light. It is not "psychic" phenomena alone which require this condition ; is it not also demanded for the impression of images on a photographic plate? Have not certain chemical combinations in the laboratory to be made in the dark? And does not the night bring about changes in the functions of organisms, animal as well as vegetable? It is no wonder, therefore, to a man of science who knows these facts, if the mediumist, metapsychic, or bio-dynamic force (the name is of no importance) is inhibited or neutralised by light, especially for the production of the important phenomena of materialisation.

Even as seen in the light of historical analogy we may find justification for the rigid character of spiritistic phenomena ; the table, the dark cabinet, &c., are like the earthen pot of Papias, with regard to our modern locomotive, or as the rude electrstatic machine of a hundred and fifty years ago in comparison with our present stupendous dynamos.

Some make the objection (and I was once one of them) that mediums, beginning with Eusapia, should be subjected to more scientific vigilance, by surrounding them with recording apparatus to register every movement, to measure their efforts, to take away every doubt as to fraud. I must premise that the traditional technique of the sittings being accepted as necessary, the "control" entrusted to two attentive observers, one on each side, appears to be sufficient ; the spiritists maintain this, and Eusapia requires it. Barzini and I did not find it difficult to hold and watch the lady's hands and feet ; after a little practice we learned to hold these extremities without allowing them to escape, and at the same time to watch her head (which was always visible) and to be attentive to the phenomena. It is not every one who succeeds in this multiple work, muscular, mental, and tactile, but I am certain that every time that the control devolved on me, Eusapia has never, except for one or two naïve attempts, carried out the supposed trick of substitution of hands (by which, moreover, not one-twentieth part of her phenomena could be explained) ; nor could she, as some have absurdly supposed, caress my forehead, pull my moustache, or sound trumpets with her feet.

Moreover, the "control" adopted at spiritistic séances is somewhat ridiculous; it tires those who carry it out, and certainly hinders Eusapia from giving new and spontaneous manifestations of her mediumship, which might be very fine. I should like to have the more remarkable phenomena of materialisation with the medium at liberty; I have had them, and very surprising ones, with Eusapia fixed and bound, but who knows what energy she might be able to externalise if she were left to the automatism of her sub-consciousness?

It is true that every modification of the habitual technique is a check on deceit, but it is also an impediment and sometimes a complete hindrance to mediumistic phenomena. Those who demand scientific "control" do not consider that mediumship, whatever be its origin and nature, is not a mechanical function like that of a physical apparatus; it is based on psychism, and it cannot be claimed that the actions of automatism, or of the sub-consciousness will take place under fixed conditions to which only a machine of iron or of wood can be indifferent. It is as though a living physiologist should claim to study a functional act of the living and thinking person, such as the poetic or amorous frenzy by surrounding the poet who creates, or the lover who loves, with his complicated paraphernalia of "control." Is it likely that he would accomplish the end aimed at by an experiment so ill-conceived?

No; physical facts have their proper conditions for production, but they cannot be discharged at our pleasure, like an arquebus or an electrical pile.

In about thirty sittings I have seen Paladino perform several hundred phenomena. One or two sittings turned out, it is true, not very interesting, especially to those who, being acquainted with her powers and having been present at the simpler and more elementary phenomena (movements of the table, touching with invisible hands, &c.), expected and hoped for higher and more complex manifestations. But there were sittings, though rare even for Eusapia, which compensated for all the tiresomeness of the long evenings passed in fruitless and unsatisfactory waiting, in which the summit of Paladino's mediumship was reached, and we witnessed the exceptional phenomena of full materialisations, of veritable apparitions.

In general, however, all who are merely curious, and many students of metapsychic facts, have not patience, do not know how to *wait,* and want to see without delay the astonishing things described in spiritistic works, which they know it to be possible for Eusapia to perform. The impatience of those who form new circles, however, is harmful to the spontaneity of the phenomena, because, although transformed into mechanical or material action, these phenomena are bio-psychical in their origin ; the more important ones occur especially when they are not asked for or expected. Contrary to what is often said about Paladino's sittings, those have to take place in conditions of the greatest mental calmness.

Moreover, the medium has not always the power to do what is desired of her, whence arises that tendency to conscious or unconscious simulation, about which such an outcry is made ; while, by reason of her scanty education, Eusapia has very little inventive faculty, even in her sub-consciousness, which must, according to my observations, almost always act by receiving from the superior or lucid portion of the consciousness the idea or the impulse to be acted upon or of the direction to be given to such impulse. The medium, being a psychically abnormal person (a "hysteric"), is suggestionable, and very often certain phenomena are performed immediately after they have been spoken of or asked for by the sitters ; in such cases the idea of the phenomenon, perceived by the waking or semi-waking consciousness of Eusapia, descends or (so to speak) plunges into her sub-consciousness, in which is elaborated the still unknown bio-psychic dynamism of mediumship, and from thence it is released and emerges in the form of mechanical action at a distance, of luminous or materialisation phenomena, &c.

In this connection it is important to define the mental state of the medium during the phenomena. I will only say here that whereas for the minor phenomena (raps, movements of the table, levitations, &c.), Eusapia can be seen to be awake and attentive, although very soon her attention is restricted to certain groups of perceptions, yet in the case of the major phenomena, those of greater significance in the spiritist doctrine and more novel to the observer (such as strong action at a distance, the apparition of forms or phantasms) it is necessary that her consciousness should he obscured in "trance," and her will in suspense. It is only then that we have the automatic discharge of the energies which we call mediumistic, accumulated in her nervous centres ; then only do we enter into the mysterious and surprising region of true "spiritism." In the work which I have promised and announced, I shall give all the fruits of my observations and experiments on the physio-psychological state of the medium, on the symptoms and gradations of her "trance," and on the various auto-suggestive processes put into operation by Eusapia during the sittings ; I hope to show that in order to thoroughly understand and appreciate metapsychical phenomena we have to be psychologists, and not merely physicists or photographers or dilettantes in curiosities and the "marvellous."

The mediumistic phenomena of Eusapia, as I have observed them, are very various and intense in the physical sphere, but very poor in the intellectual one ; and this, for me, is a great blow to the spiritistic doctrine, since the scientific conclusion to be drawn from it, though little acceptable to systematic spiritists, is that the phenomena are due exclusively to the action of the mediums and are proportional to the psychic or sub-psychic elements existing in their brain by individual acquisition or by cumulative heredity.

To reduce somewhat to order the intricate tangle of spiritistic psychic manifestations, many classifications have been adopted. Some are merely empirical, grouping the phenomena according to their outward characters without pretending to touch their inward nature. Crookes commenced in this prudent way when he set forth by "classes" his famous experiments of 1870–74 ; Gibier followed in his studies on Slade, and so did the Milan Commission of 1892, and De Rochas in his studies on Eusapia, Aksakoff, and Gyel in the excellent synthetic *rësume* of spiritism, &c. Other classifications are of a theoretical nature, or attempts to arrange the phenomena according to their inward nature, whether real or conjectural ; and among those the first place is merited by that daring attempt (yet, in my opinion, lacking in positive basis) of the great psychist, F. W. H. Myers (*Human Personality*). Myers has achieved by his studies and by his devotion a monumental and admirable work ; but he has claimed too much in trying to connect the most "spiritual" and exceptional facts of "spiritism" with the most elementary facts of biology and psychology ; he has not succeeded in filling up the enormous, dark, and still unfathomable gulf which separates and distinguishes them from each other.

I also shall try elsewhere to construct a co-ordinated and complete scheme of mediumistic nomenclature ; but I shall take care to keep on the firm ground of observation. In those articles I shall content myself with grouping in a clear and easily comprehensible manner the phenomena of Eusapia which have been observed by myself. I do not deny that Eusapia, like other mediums, may have given other and more decided manifestations of her rnediumship in sittings at which I was not present, and may in the future give new and different ones, and perhaps more convincing in favour of the "spiritistic" hypothesis. Nor do I deny that she may, in further experiments or sittings, and before other observers, show herself incapable of producing the phenomena witnessed and verified by me ; not so much because Eusapia is not always in possession of equal bio-psychic-dynamic powers, as because the study of mediumistic forces, but just commenced, has in store for science surprises which cannot be foreseen.

* * *

The greater number of those who at present interest themselves in spiritism, either for or against, have been greatly impressed by the movements of the table produced by Paladino ; the spiritists, and those who consider that the existence of "psychical forces" is now proved, use them to demonstrate the reality of these forces ; the incredulous, to bring up all the objections and doubts, and all the more or less inconsistent hypotheses which have been put forth in explanation of this very evident and real phenomenon. But this typtokinesis, to give it a Greek name, forms the ABC of Paladino's manifestations ; and when one has had the chances which I have had to witness the apparition of phantasms, the phenomenon of the moving table, while preserving its high importance as an objective fact which can be actually verified by photography, loses much of its striking character so much wondered at by the anti-psychists, and takes its proper place among the much more numerous and complex objective or physical effects of Eusapia's mediumship. I shall rapidly review the principal classes of phenomena, giving little more than the names, and keeping to the scheme of classilication most commonly adopted in reports and treatises on psychical subjects. But every classification has the fault of artificiality, and thus the following groupings must be understood rather as expressing their outward form of production than as denoting their substantial dynamical affinities ; such a division according to intrinsic character can only be made after longer and more mature experience.

The first class includes mechanical phenomena, with production of motion in objects by contact with the person of the medium, but with effects disproportionate to tho expenditure of ordinary nervo-muscular force on the part of the medium herself. Maxwell calls them "parakinesis," and Eusapia produces them both in darkness and in the light, always, be it understood, under secure "control."

1. *Oscillations and movements of the table without significance.* These are the initial and elementary facts of all the complicated phenomena of spiritism. I have felt them under my hands, and have also seen them with my eyes, hundreds of times, since from beginning to end of each séance with Eusapia the table is constantly, every little while, shaking, raising itself on one side or the other, oscillating, and then becoming quiet again without any-

thing else happening.

2. *Movements and beatings of the table having significance.* These also are very frequent, and those corresponding to the conventional language used by Paladino (two blows "no," three blows "yes," &c.), regulate for the most part the proceedings of the sitting, order or consent to changes in the chain, ask for modifications of the light, &c. It is true that in Eusapia's séances this typtology (which we never encouraged in the purely spiritistic sense) is reduced to very little in comparison with the marvellous communications of a personal or of a philosophical-social character giver by other mediums. In compensation, Eusapia's table has a very rich languago which I may call mimetic, which has been well described by L. Barzini, and which resembles the mimicry of a child.

3. *Complete lifting of the table (improperly called "levitation" by empirical spiritists).* It is frequently seen at the sittings that tho table is completely lifted from the floor when the hands of the medium, placed upon it, do not make any effort whatever, and cannot contribute to it ; and the phenomenon has several times been recorded by photography in an incontestable manner ; I shall reproduce some of the photographs in my book.

4. *Movements of various objects barely touched by the hands or body of the medium.* Eusapia, laying her hands lightly on chairs or other articles of furniture, and objects of various weights, succeeds in imparting to them movements of displacement of lifting, or of rotation on their own axis, which are not to be explained with certainty by the very light pressure exercised by her.

5. *Movement, undulations, and swellings of the curtain of the cabinet.* I place this very curious phenomenon here because the black curtains of the cabinet are as a rule in

contact with the medium's seat, and often full over her back. The curtains move, swell outwards from within the cabinet, come forward, draw back, open and close, without Eusapia being able to do this with her hands and feet, which are always kept under strict control.

6. *Movements and swellings out of the medium's clothes.* This phenomenon, upon which the Cambridge Commission erroneously based a proclamation that Eusapia cheated, is, on the contrary, by our direct observation, genuine ; it takes place mostly in full light and while Eusapia's feet are closely watched ; the impression formed is as though supernumerary limbs, invisible but palpable, were formed under the medium's skirt.

The second class is only the first in more perfect form, or mechanical effects produced without any contact with the person of the medium, at a distance which may vary from an inch or two to a yard or more. They are the most disputed, because they are incomprehensible according to the ordinary laws of physics, which teach that a mechanical force must act directly on the resistance offered by material bodies ; and yet this telekinesis is one of the things most frequently seen at Paladino's sittings. I will mention summarilly the principal phenomena of this class.

7. *Oscillations and movements of the table without contact.* We have verified this several times ; all of us, including Etisapia, raised our hands from the surface of the table, and the latter continued to give proof of its ability to move by itself.

8. *Independent liftings of the table.* This is a phenomenon one prefers to photograph. We saw in full light the table raised to the height of our heads while we were standing up in the middle of the room. I have also been present at veritable *pas seuls* of the table by full gas-light,

when the medium was secured within the cabinet.

9. *Undulations, swellings, and movements of the curtain of the cabinet.* These happen also when the medium is evidently at a distance—for instance, when she is lying down and bound firmly within the cabinet ; one would say that invisible persons were raising the curtain with their hand drawing it one way to open it and another way to close it, &c.

10. *Movements occasioned in material objects by the hands being voluntarily turned towards them, but at a distance.* This impressive phenomenon usually occurs in the light and at the close of the sitting. It is veritable externalisation of motricity, as described by Colonel de Rochas ; and Barzini has given a very effective description of it.

11. *Spontaneous movement and displacement of various objects at various distances from the medium.* Seats are seen and heard to move, also tables, utensils, musical instruments, &e. ; in short, the whole apparatus usual at spiritistic séances, at such a distance from the medium as to render absurd the hypothesis of deception I have seen such phenomena occur oven at a distance of two or three yards.

12. *Bringing of distant objects on to the table.* These are phenomena in which Eusapia appears to take great pleasure. Objects of every kind, even when placed (and this is always to be understood) in positions easily verifiable, acquire under her mediumistic influence an apparent power of self-movement, as though they were alive. I shall narrate elsewhere some astonishing examples. I ought, however, to say that very often there was some connection between the objects so moved and the curtains of the cabinet, which perform a very important part in the phenomena of Paladino, as though invisible hands were behind them.

13. *Displacement of the seats of the experimenters.* This is another phenomenon highly pleasing to that jester "John King." Several times I was pulled violently on my chair, back towards the cabinet, to receive special manifestations of a personal character. Sometimes we felt our chairs pulled from beneath us, &c.

14. *Appropriate movements of mechanical instruments placed at a distance.* These really multitudinous phenomena relate, for instance, to the apparently spontaneous setting in action of musical instruments (mandolin, zither, pianoforte, trumpet, &c.), or other small mechanical articles (carillons, metronome, dynamometer, &c.), at a distance from Eusapia. These occurred at almost every sitting. Here I may mention the mysterious opening and closing of the electric circuit of the lights by means of unperceived manipulations of the pear-shaped switches contained in the pocket of one of the sitters.

The third class of mechanical phenomena relates to the alteration of the weight of bodies. I ought, however, to state that to me they seemed to be the least certain of the phenomena, although other observers guarantee their authenticity.

15. *Spontaneous changes of weight in a scale.* I have not seen the phenomenon of the letter-weigher, reported as genuine by Colonel de Rochas ; but we were present at the oscillation in the arm of a weighing-machine when it was not visibly pressed by Eusapia, though she was near to the platform ; this phenomenon, however, appeared doubtful.

16. *Change of weight in the body of the medium.* As to this also, though it occurred under my eyes, I have no scientific certainty, and I only mention it to encourage students to make further researches.

17. *Raising of the medium's body in the air.* This is the real "levitation" which is narrated to have been performed by certain saints. Home was levitated up to the ceiling! It sometimes happens that Eusapia is lifted bodily, together with her chair, and, to her great alarm, deposited on the table. I have only once seen this "miracle," contrary to the law of gravitation, and had the impression that it was genuine at the beginning, but was unconsciously aided in its completion by the two guardians ; it would be well to see it again and study it carefully.

A curious class which has been little studied up to now is that of the mediumistic effects which I will call those of thermal radiation ; it consists of few but interesting phenomena.

18. *Wind from the cabinet.* This is very frequent, and is felt at almost every sitting ; it is a veritable current of air, which comes from within the cabinet and behind the medium.

19. *Intense cold.* This is usually announced by the two controllers, and is the prelude to many manifestations: on certain evenings it becomes perceptible to all the persons forming the chain. It may perhaps be symbolical of the cold of the "sepulchres" which open to let the "defunct" come forth. Certainly it is impressive and is not hallucinatory.

20. *Radiations from the head and body of the medium.* On putting the hand to Eusapia's head, especially where she has a breach in the bone caused by an old fall, and sometimes also at her hands, one feels a sensible "breath," now warm, now cool. I need not say that this phenomenon (of which I shall speak later at length) is significant as regards the hypothesis of new nervous forces.

The class of acoustic phenomena is already partly comprised in the first three, since very often movements at a distance are rendered perceptible by noises, sounds, rubbing over the floor, &c., of the objects and instruments set in motion. But there are also other special phenomena of this class.

21. *Blows, raps, and other sounds in the table.* Of the famous "raps" of Anglo-American spiritism hundreds have been heard at Eusapia's sittings. Some have the intensity of blows delivered by a powerful but invisible fist. Others (and not the least mysterious) take place in the joints of the wood.

22. *Blows and raps at a distance from the rnedium.* These are very often heard within the cabinet, or on the seats of the two guardians and their neighbours, on the furniture, on the walls, in the cabinet, &c.

23. *Sounds of musical instruments.* I have already alluded to these; we have had them under such conditions as to exclude all action of visible and tangible hands; the trumpets emit their harsh sound in the air, the strings of the mandolins and zithers vibrate, the keys of the pianoforte give detached notes; and all this without anyone visibly touching them. But they are never really musical sounds, in my experience, nor harmonic chords, still less airs of some melody; at the best they are rhythms in measured time.

24. *Sounds of hands, feet, &c.* In various cases the clapping of hands is heard, either behind the curtain or in the air of the room. Once or twice we seemed to hear footsteps within the Cabinet.

25. *Sounds of human voices.* This is a very rare phenomenon, and consists in hearing the "voices" of the discarnate. I only perceived it once under conditions

which were not convincing ; but this is not the place to relate the particulars of my extraordinary spiritistic adventure (the apparent materialisation of a disincarnate being who was very dear to me).

I pass on to a class of manifestations not less impressive and which, according to spiritists, go to prove the action of occult "intelligences" by producing lasting effects on inert matter. Eusapia, being uneducated, gives very few of these phenomena.

26. *Mysterious signs left at distance.* These consist in signs or marks found on the table, on the cuffs of the sitters, or on the wall, and seem to bo made with pencil. They do not appear to me sufficiently certain to merit attention.

27. *Direct writing.* This is supposed to be writing made directly by the "spirits" without the apparent action of hands, whether done with visible writing instruments (pencil or crayon) or without. But Eusapia is illiterate and cannot write, and in all the sittings at which I was present only two or three times did there appear signs of writing which might be taken for badly formed letters. The spirits evoked by the Apulian countrywoman seemed also to be very ignorant ; and this appears to me to be a very grave objection to the spiritistic hypothesis.

28. *Impression in plastic substances.* This is a favourite phenomenon with students of psychical matters, and Eusapia gives good examples of it, although sometimes under circumstances suggestive of doubt. They are impressions of fingers, palms, hands, fists, foot, and also of faces, generally in full profile or half profile ; those faces have a certain resemblance to a Eiasapia grown old, and in fact arc said to be reproductions of the face of "John King," her father in a former life. At our sittings we ob-

tained many such impressions, and as to the greater part of them, we are certain that there was no deception.

29. *Apports.* These figure as phenomena of the very foremost rank in the history and doings of the most famous mediums. The phenomenon is one of the greatest significance for the spiritist doctrine of the disaggregation and reconstitution of matter, for it consists in the unexpected appearance on the table or in the room of objects (such as flowers, branches, leaves, iron nails, coins, stones, &c.) coming from a distance and penetrating through doors and walls. This phenomenon was reported two or three times during our sittings, but I frankly confess that I was not convinced of it, which does not imply that under better observation it might not be real also in the case of Paladino, as it seems to have been through the agency of other mediums.

30. *Knotting and unknotting of a piece of string, cords, &c., in the dark cabinet as well as on the person of Eusapia.* I have seen this phenomenon on several occasions.

We now come to the higher ranges of phenomena, to those which constitute the true basis of spiritism ; I refer to the category of materialisations. This is a case of creation *ex nihilo*, by the use of the vital fluid or spirit of the medium, of forms more or less organised, having the physical characteristics assigned by us to matter, that is, of being resistant to the sense of touch and muscular pressure (tangible), and of being sometimes endowed with light of their own (luminous), but for the most part only capable of arresting exterior rays of light (thus rendering themselves visible).

The first sub-class is that of solid materialisations, which I will call mediumistic stereosis or plasmation.

31. *Touching, feeling, and grasping by invisible hands.*

These form a very common phenomenon at the dark séances, or by a faint light, or a red light ; and they are really human hands which touch, press, grasp, pull, push, pat lightly, strike, pull the sitters' beards or hair, take off their spectacles, &c. Some of those to whom such contacts were new have been caused to shudder, and really the first time they cause quite an impression.

32. *Organisations of solid forms having the characteristics of human limbs.* These are usually hands, arms, shoulders(?), and even heads, which are felt behind the curtain, and seem to be pieces or fragments of a being which is in process of formation ; occasionally they give the tangible impression of the whole of a person. On being grasped through the curtain they usually withdraw hasily ; but sometimes they remain long enough to allow themselves to be handled, especially the faces. The invisible mouth also makes movements indicative of kissing, biting, &c., usually under cover of the stuff.

33. *Organisation of hands, naked and distinguishable to the touch.* At certain times we felt ourselves touched by real human hands, having the character of members of a living being ; we felt the skin, the warmth, the movable fingers, &c. On grasping them one felt the impression of hands dissolving away, as though composed of semi-fluid substance.

34. *Complicated actions of materialised forms, tangible but invisible.* These hands, arms, heads, and half-persons, while remaining imperceptible to the sight even on looking into the cabinet, behind the curtains, advance towards the sitters, touch and feel them, embrace, grasp, draw them nearer, or push them away, caress and kiss them, with all the movements of living and real persons. They also execute still more complex actions, both in the shade of the cabinet and in front of it, with the interpo-

sition of the curtain, which is swelled out and projected for the purpose on to the table or towards the seats of those near, even though out of the chain ; and also in full freedom in the very midst of the sitters, so that some of those present feel themselves invisibly pushed against, pressed, their pockets searched, &c. This last astonishing manifestation, of those previously mentioned, I am quite certain occurred very rarely, and only in complete darkness or by a very faint light which did not allow anything to be clearly seen, so that, though I was present one evening when it occurred, I cannot remove from my mind all uncertainty and should require fuller and more convincing demonstration. Some of those present believed that they recognised and "identified" these invisible forms, by means of impressions of touch and feeling through the curtains. But, in the cases at which I was present, the identification does not sustain, as I shall show, a critical analysis of the psychological origin of the phenomenon ; the latter, however, remains real and authentic, though incomprehensible.

I collect into one small group the elementary luminous phenomena, self-visible or visible by exterior light, but not organised.

35. *Appearance of luminous points.* These are the celebrated "spirit lights" ; Eusapia produces them from time to time, but not with the intensity of other mediums whom I have seen. They are indefinable glow-lights, sometimes like very bright globules of light, sometimes veritable "tongues of fire," like those figured on the heads of the Apostles. They have not been photographed, as far as I know ; but they are very evident, sometimes multiple, and running together into one ; it is impossible as well as absurd for those who have once seen them, to compare them with artificial phosphores-

cent effects, not to speak of identifying them with the latter.

36. *Appearances of whitish clouds or mists.* These do not seem to be endowed with light of their own, since they can only be discerned in a dim light, outside the curtains, or within the cabinet ; sometimes they surround Eusapia's head, or rise over her body when she lies down inside the cabinet.

I place the visible materialisations last, because they appear to be formed by a very subtle substance or matter emanating from the person of the medium and composed of particles or molecules which obstruct ordinary light ("teleplastic").

37. *Formation of dark prolongations of the body of the medium.* These are the supernumerary members seen and described by all those who had previously experimented with Paladino. Visible in half-light or in very faint light, and when the actual hands of Eusapia are also in full view and well guarded, those neo-plastic appendages perform many of the phenomena above described (touching and feeling of those near, blows on the chairs, movement of objects, &c.)

38. *Forms having the appearance of arms and hands coming out of the cabinet.* This manifestation is not rare, and has been already mentioned by those who were present at previous sittings with Eusapia. Being shortsighted I was not always able to see them distinctly, but my perception, even when indistinct, has always corresponded with what has been seen more clearly by others present who have been endowed with better sight.

39. *Appearance of hands.* These are among the more common and recognised spiritistic manifestations. The hands usually appear with indistinct or evanescent out-

lines, of a whitish colour, almost transparent, and with elongated fingers. I have perceived them very clearly every time that I was in a position favourable for seeing them; and they were certainly not the medium's hands, which were simultaneously watched, and also visible to all, above the table.

40. *Appearance of obscure forms of indeterminate character or not very evident.* These are "incomplete materialisations." Sometimes there are seen, advancing and disappearing in the half light, black globes (heads?), indefinable shadowy appendages (arms? fists?); sometimes shadows with crooked profiles which may be conjectured to be bearded ("John King"); and again on the semi-luminous background there appear blackish shapes, flat, and seeming as though transparent, strangely formed, and gesticulating in an uncouth manner. They manifested to me in particular at the sittings of 1901 and 1902, and I perceived them so distinctly (as confirmed by my companions) that I was able to draw them one by one.

41. *Appearances of forms having determinate and personal characteristics, unknown to any of the sitters.* We are now at the end, because these are the "complete materialisations" and constitute the apex of Eusapia's mediumship up to the present (other mediums, including Florence Cook and Mme. d'Espérance, have given much more marvellous and truly incredible ones).

I have seen those supreme phenomena a few times only, for they are rare events in Eusapia's mediumship. They are well-delineated faces, heads and half-busts of personages, mostly unknown, not recognised by anyone present, or who are identified and named by taking advantage of the notions belonging to the traditional history of spiritism. If this is so, I must have seen the same phantasms which the celebrated Sir William Crookes saw, and, moreover, had under his hands ; that is to say, there re-appeared at our séances with Eusapia the spirit guide of Florence Cook, "Katie King," who, moreover, is a relative of "John King!"

42. *Appearance of forms having a personality known to one of the sitters.* Besides seeing some personal forms tangibly materialised, I must also have been present at a real spirit evocation! On this occasion the apparition was somewhat doubtfully identified and named by living members of his family present at the sitting ; but with regard to myself, I did not gain from this extraordinary event in my "spiritistic" experience that impression of obvious certainty which the man of science, the psychologist who studies this very new branch of science, and is habituated to the rules of the strict positive method, is obliged to impose upon himself and has the right to claim from others.

I do not desire to dwell at present on this part of Paladino's phenomena ; the space which has been assigned to me will not permit of descriptions or discusions, but only of a pure and simple synthetic *résumé* of my personal experiences.

Thus, in the phenomena in which Paladino's mediumship manifests itself, we have, according to my provisional scheme, nine classes and thirty-nine orders of manifestations ; I may possibly have forgotten one or two, and perhaps have grouped together several which ought to have been classed separately ; certainly I did not see all that were possible, and other observers may add some which are unknown to me. All this is very different from the simple lifting of the table, or the trick of exchanging hands or withdrawing the feet.

The Naples Sittings of 1908
Individual Conclusions of the Investigators, Made as an Addendum to Their Report to the Society for Psychical Research

By HEREWARD CARRINGTON, W. W. BAGGALLY, EVERARD FIELDING

FINAL NOTE BY HEREWARD CARRINGTON

As a result of the ten sittings held by us at Naples, November 21st. — December 15th, 1908,—being the ten séances attended by me, I beg to record my absolute conviction of the reality of at least some of the phenomena ; and the conviction, amounting in my own mind to complete certainty, that the results witnessed by were not due to fraud or trickery on the part of Eusapia. It would be impossible to impart this feeling of certainty to others, since that could only he obtained by a series of personal sittings ; and the critic must depend for his conviction upon our record of the séances,—as we have had hitherto to depend upon the records of others. This is a very different thing from attending the séances oneself. Just as one can only gain a correct idea of a fraudulent spiritualistic séance by attending it in person, so, I think, can one only reach a definite conclusion in favour of the phenomena by attending genuine séances. The curious fact recorded by Mr. Fielding that the incidents seemed to roll off our minds and that we lapsed back into skepticism on each occasion, until we had held four or five séances, was noticed by all of us ; and it is only when one is controlling the medium oneself, and when one has absolute confidence in the controllers on the other side, that one reaches that state of complete conviction which it would be impossible to reach in any other manner.

One or two of the phenomena occurred under what I was forced to regard as ideal conditions of control. The touches during the latter part of Séance VI. were among these, when I was holding the medium's left hand in her lap, and controlling practically the whole of her body, while Mr. Baggally was controlling the right hand on the table, and these were the cases that convinced me finally and conclusively that genuine phenomena occurred, though I could see no definite reason for refusing credence to many of the phenomena of the previous séances. Still, there is a difference between intellectual and emotional conviction, and, whereas the first of these states had been reached by the end of the second séance, the second did not result until the sixth séance, as I have said. Never were the two degrees more clearly marked than on this occasion in my own mind ; and it is probable that the second of the two stages will only be reached by the majority when psychical science assumes a more definitely experimental form. Thus, on several occasions, I verified my own control and found it perfect ; I also verified the control of my colleague. I then stretched my disengaged hand out towards the curtain, saying, "Now, if I am touched under these conditions, I shall consider the phenomenon definitely and finally proved." On several such occasions, I did receive touches apparently of hands, and I was consequently forced to the conclusion that these phenomena were absolutely genuine, and not the results of fraud on the part of Eusapia.

June 1909

Final Note by W. W. Baggally

On reading through the shorthand notes I find that 470 phenomena are recorded as having taken place during the course of the eleven séances. Of these phenomena:

> 305 took place when members of the S.P.R. Committee controlled;
>
> 144 took place when a non-member and a member of the S.P.R. Committee controlled;
>
> 21 took place when two non-members controlled;
>
> 470 I have classed as phenomena in connection with the séance table, the complete levitations only, excluding the raps on it and its tilts and rockings, as, although some of these occurred under extremely good evidential conditions, the majority were non-evidential.

At some of the séances the phenomena succeeded each other so rapidly that it was not possible to record them all, and consequently their number is largely understated.

For the strict purposes of the S.P.R. investigation, perhaps only the phenomena which occurred when the members of the Committee alone controlled should be taken into account. At the time that these took place (except on the occasion when a current of air issued from Eusapia's head) the medium sat outside the cabinet with her back to the curtains, and a member of the

S.P.R. Committee sat on each side of her controlling her handa and feet. These 305 phenomena may be explained by one of four hypotheses:

(1) That they were all fraudulent.
(2) That they were all genuine.
(3) That some were genuine and the others fraudulent.
(4) That some were genuine and the others not proved to be either genuine or fraudulent.

I proceed to consider these hypotheses in their order.

(1) If all the phenomena were fraudulent they must have been produced either by the liberation of one of Eusapia's hands or feet, after she had carried out a substitution ; or, when she was not able to resort to this method, owing to her hands or feet being too far apart, by the removal of one of her hands or feet from the hand or foot of the controller (he, after such a removal, continuing under the impression that he still felt her hand or foot in contact with his own), or by the use of her head or other part of her body, or some mechanism concealed about her person, or by the help of a accomplice.

Now it is a remarkable fact that (excluding the three occasions on which substitutions of hands took place, which were followed by no phenomena), Eusapia was not detected resorting to any fraudulent methods during the production of any of the 305 phenomena. I cannot accept the theory that the members of the Committee were suffering from a collective hallucination. The fact that they were able to verify that the objects which they saw brought out of the cabinet remained outside at the termination of the sitting is sufficient to disprove it. Taking into consideration the manner of the control, that no mechanism was found on the medium's person, that no accomplice was present, and also that I do not include among the 470 phenomena the occasion when Eusapia made a substitution of hands and then brought the curtain forward and placed it on the table, because, in the view of F. and C., the incident did not purport to be supernormal.

The non-detection of fraud also applies to all the other phenomena of the eleven sittings which are not included in the above 305.

The three S.P.R. investigators were men who had been accustomed for years to the investigation of so-called physical phenomena of every variety, and who had detected fraud after fraud. I find it impossible to believe that Eusapia could have been able to practise trickery constantly during the many hours that the séances lasted and remain undetected.

(2) As regards the second hypothesis, "that all the phenomena were genuine," I cannot positively assert that this is correct. The chances of occasional mal-observation on the part of the investigators should not be excluded. Eusapia was detected practising the trick of substitution on three occasions ; it is therefore possible that she may have been able, unobserved, to liberate one of her hands or feet on other occasions, and by this means to produce fraudulently some of the phenomena ; but neither my colleagues nor I had proof that she resorted to fraud in the production of any one of the phenomena.

(3) Regarding the third hypothesis, "that some of the phenomena were genuine and the others fraudulent," the second part of this is negatived by the remark just made ; it only then remains to consider the first part "that some of the phenomena were genuine." On this point I feel that I can speak with assurance, though I am

aware of the difficulty of imparting to a critic, by a mere description, the same conviction of the supernormal character of the particular phenomena in question as I gained from personal observation. One cannot easily accept as genuine phenomena which appear to contravene the known laws of Nature, and before doing so, one must be assured that by no possibility could they have been produced by normal means. A knowledge of the conjuring art is obviously of great use in enabling an investigator to judge whether a medium is practising fraud or not, and two members of the S.P.R. Committee possessed this knowledge. I have already mentioned the only normal methods which under the circumstances Eusapia, in my opinion, could have used for the fraudulent production of the phenomena, viz., the unobserved liberation and use of one of her hands or feet, the unobserved use of her head or other part of her body, or of some mechanism concealed about her person. The help of a confederate need not be considered, as the séances took place in our own room with locked doors.

It has been suggested to us that possibly M., the stenographer, assisted the medium as a confederate. To this suggestion I would reply that M. is a gentleman whose services F. engaged without previously informing Eusapia that a stenographer would be present at the investigation, and that he had never met the medium before. During the whole time that the séances at which I was present lasted, M.'s face was lit by the lamp which he used for the purpose of taking the notes. His face was clearly visible to the controllers, and therefore his position in the séance room was never lost sight of. The table at which he sat was several feet away from the end of the séance table furthest away from the medium. He never moved from his table except when he was asked to come near Eusapia, the better to witness a few of the phenomena.

As regards the possibility of a confederate gaining access into the cabinet by a trap door, I may say that I examined the interior of the cabinet and found that the floor was made of tiles closely cemented together. The walls were at right angles to each other ; one consisting of thick masonry gave on to the street ; the other of thin masonry, brick or plaster, separated the séance room from my bedroom. There was no trap door.

If certain phenomena take place when both hands of tbe medium are distinctly seen, above, or quietly resting on, the séance table, or both hands are clearly seen when being held by the controllers, and at the same time her body is in view down to her feet, while the controllers are assured, by tactile examination or by their sense of sight, that no mechanism is being brought into play, and when it is certain that there is no accomplice ; if certain phenomena, I say, take place under the above conditions, which seem to exclude all conceivable normal means of producing the phenomena, there is then a strong presumption that they are produced supernormally, and it was the phenomena which occurred under these strictly test conditions that first convinced me of this. I will now give a few examples of such phenomena.

I have already *[in his note on Séance VII, inset following.]* recounted in detail the remarkable movement of Eusapia's dress.

> I attach great importance to the phenomenon that occurred at the very beginning of the séance, viz, the *"gonfiamento"* or swelling out of Eusapia's dress which took place before and after F. had placed the little stool on the floor on the left side

of the medium in order to try and repeat the experiment which he had witnessed with the late M. Curie and his colleagues of the Institut Général Psychologique in Paris. If the stringent conditions under which these movements of Eusapia's dress took place are considered, it will be seen that this phenomenon, although not of a startling character, was of great evidential value. She had hardly sat down when she called our attention to the movement of her dress. The light had not been lowered; it was the strongest that we used at these seances—not shaded. By it I could read small print and see every object in the room clearly. The medium's hands rested quietly on the table in full view of us all, and her feet were under the strictest control of F. and C. We all watched the peculiar movement. The force under the dress made an evidently intelligent effort to reach the stool. The bulge in the garment was not a pointed one, but more like what a breeze of wind would produce. The dress did not, however, swell out *en masse*; it only did so at a certain part, as if a small balloon under the garment were pushing it towards the stool. F. felt right down the dress at the time of the bulging and not feel any hard object under it. Eusapia laughingly asked us find "la machina," and thereupon lifted her dress and petticoats. No apparatus, such as a rod, which the late Dr. Hodgson suggested have been employed by her, or an India rubber tube, through which a gust of wind could have been blown, or anything else, was found. After Eusapia had lowered her dress, the movement recommenced. After the swelling occurred the lower edge of the dress touching the floor slid towards the stool in a peculiar rnsnner, while edge repeatedly advanced and retired slowly; at each successive advance gradually diminishing the distance between it and the stool. I compared this sliding motion in my mind, at the time, to movement of a protuberance from the body of a unicellular organism. F. felt with his hand several times between the dress and the and found no attachment.

This took place at the beginning of the seventh séance, in the strongest light (unshaded) that we used from the time that I joined in the investigation, when the medium's hands were resting on the séance table in full view of all the members of the S.P.R. Committee, when her whole body was seen (I stood quite close to Eusapia intently watching her), and when her two feet were securely held by F. and C., there being no possibility of a substitution of feet nor the use of any mechanism nor attachment, as the medium showed us, at the time, that her two feet were separately held and that no mechanism was concealed under her dress ; F. felt with his hand several times, and found no attachment.

Another phenomenon which greatly impressed me was the bulging of the curtain after the conclusion of the sixth séance at about 2 am. The light had been raised to No. 1 light. Eusapia released both her hands from control and placed them on the table. They were perfectly visible to all of us. Both her feet were under control. I noticed that the curtain, which was on the medium's right, but not in contact with any part of her body, made a slight movement. I immediately realised that if the curtain bulged out at that time there could be no possibility of her being able to produce the movement by normal means without detection, as owing to the good light and to my position, I could distinctly see at the same moment her head, her two hands, her body down to her feet, and the curtain which was close to me and not touching her.

A very short time after this thought crossed my mind, and while I was intently watching Eusapia, who did not move, the curtain bulged strongly out, as if pressed from within the cabinet by a balloon. The bulge was about a foot and a half from the medium's head and on a level with it. Eusapia was examined shortly afterwards, at this séance, and no mechanism was found concealed about her body.

There was a curious parallelism between the bulges of Eusapia's dress and those of the curtains. Those that I saw were all globular in form and they did not show themselves close to the ground. The remarkable nature of these bulges should be kept in mind. When they were felt by the hand of a sitter they offered no resistance, but gave the impression of being caused by a current of air blown from behind the curtain. They were never pointed or irregular in form, as would have been the case had they been brought about by a thread attached to the curtain or by a hand or foot pushing the curtain forward. The bulges of the curtains were sometimes on a level with Eusapia's head and sometimes higher or lower. Her head was, as I have said, visible when the bulges took place.

A notable phenomenon of a different character was one that was witnessed at 11 am. after the termination of Séance XI. when Mrs. H. had ceased to control. This lady retained her seat on the left of the medium and I retained mine on her right. The other persons who had been present at the séance (with the exception of the stenographer, who remained seated at his table) had retired into C.'s room. They had left the door wide open so that the séance room was now not only lit by Light 1 (the strongest light used at the séances), but also by the light from the adjoining room which was full on. Eusapia continued in a state of semi-trance, her elbows on the table, her hands raised. She tightly closed the fist of the left hand, as if by nervous tension, and made three motions with it towards the closed door which was behind my back (I was seated between the medium and the door and had a full view of her hands and the right side of her body from her head to her foot), whereupon three loud raps were heard on the door. After this she made several gestures with her hand ; and each time raps were heard on the door, finishing with four large gestures followed by four loud raps. These raps were heard by Mrs. H. and myself. They distinctly came from the door behind me and not from where Eusapia sat in front of me. The medium then held my right hand in her right and scratched the back of my right hand with the finger nails of her left and, synchronously, a rasping sound was heard on the door. The distance between the medium's hand and the door when she made the gestures and scratched my hand was about 3 feet, and the distance between her feet and the door about 3 feet. I was much impressed by these phenomena as they were taking place, and, without leaving my seat, called F. from the other room. His note, in the stenographic report, is as follows:

> "B. called me in from the other room. I asked medium to repeat raps. It seemed as though the force were expended. She made three or four gestures and no raps followed. Then she made a final gesture and a loud rap followed. It appeared to me distinctly to come from the door beside which

I was standing. Her feet were at least three feet from the door, and her hand, as she made the gesture, did not approach within six inches of it. There was a clear space between the whole of the medium and the door."

When F. came into the séance room Eusapia did not succeed in obtaining a rap until she brought her hand within a distance of six inches from the door, whereas when I first heard the raps her hand was about 3 feet from it. F. placed himself between the medium and the door in a similar position to my own, and was thus able to confirm the fact, which I have stated, that Eusapia's hands could be clearly seen, in the excellent light, that the whole of her right side was in view down to her feet, and that the loud rap that he heard, like those that I heard, came distinctly from the door and not from where the medium sat.

The apparently supernormal agency was not only able to produce percussive and other sounds at a distance from Eusapia's body, and to move comparatively light objects, such as her dress or the curtains of the cabinet, but could also affect heavy objects, as was shown by many of the complete levitations of the séance table which occurred when one of my colleagues of the S.P.R. Committee and I controlled. I would refer the reader to the complete levitations which took place during Séance IX. at 10.11, 10.16, and 10.17 p.m. *[see inset here following from session notes by Baggally]*

> The numerous complete levitations of the table at this séance afforded further evidence of the existence of a telekinetic force exercised by Easapia. The light was sufficiently good to enable us to see

her hands and legs at the moment that some of the levitations took place, and no suspicious movement on her part was detected. Her feet were also under control, and could not been inserted under the table legs, and the hand of one of controllers was on both her knees. The complete levitations, the swelling out of the medium's dress already referred to, and the bulging of the curtains of the cabinet, afforded me the strongest evidence thus far obtained by us for the existence of this force, owing to the excellent test conditious under which I observed them.

During the production of these phenomena, and when the objects were outside the cabinet, the movement could be watched from the moment of its initiation. If this movement were due to a supernormal force, as the test conditions under which it was produced suggest, it is not impossible that this same force is also at work when objects are brought out of the cabinet, although their motion is not then perceptible,—if the test conditions in this latter case are equally severe. This supposed force appears to be able to attract matter, as when the medium held her hands above the table (her feet being under control), the table was completely levitated, with all four feet, from the ground. It appears also to repel it, as when she placed her hands below the table, not touching it (her feet being under control), the table rose same manner.

The movements of the little stool which was placed on the outside the cabinet, on her left, at a distance of three feet from her left hand and two and a-half feet from her left foot, illustrated the double action of this force. When she made a motion of her hand high above the stool, as if pushing it away from her, it retired; and when she made the motion, also high above stool, as if drawing it towards her, it advanced in her direction.

At the time these motions were taking place I was sure I had a good control of her left leg. My right foot was not only against her left, but the whole length of my right leg was between hers and the stool. The light was sufficient to enable us to see the little stool as it moved in different directions.

The strongest Light, No. 1, was then on: the medium's hands were plainly visible in such a position that she could not make use of them for raising the table, and at the same time a space was seen by C. and myself between the table legs and the dress of the medium on either side of her. As an additional precaution I had my right hand across her two knees, which remained motionless during the levitation. All the above phenomena occurred under these stringent test conditions. I am therefore convinced that Eusapia did not (for their production) make use of her hands, or her feet, or any part of her body ; neither did she resort to any mechanical means, nor was she assisted by a confederate, and I am compelled to ascribe those phenomena to some supernormal cause.

So far I have only treated of phenomena which were due to the action of some force of a telekinetic nature. My mind did not, *a priori,* reject the possibility of its existence owing to the fact of its newness to me, but that this force should he able to manifest itself as tangible matter and assume an organic form like a hand, capable of grasping, was a phenomenon of such a complex nature that I was not able to give it acceptance with equal ease. The phenomena, however, that I am about to describe, although lacking in one of the specific test conditions (inasmuch as the lower part of the medium's body was not in view at the time of their occurrence), offered me strong evidence that this force did materialise itself, to use a spiritualistic term, and did assume the form of a hand.

During the time that I controlled Eusapia, at the séances, I was certain that the hand that I had in contact with mine was her right hand (or her left hand as the case might be), as I continually assured myself of the fact by feeling the relative position of her thumb and palm, and also that it was a living hand by the responses that it gave to my pressure. The controller who sat on the other side of the medium was equally certain that the hand that he had in contact with his own was her other hand, for the same reasons. I had, therefore, the assurance that it was not one of Eusapia's hands which issued from the cabinet and occasionally grasped me.

This assurance was greatly increased at the eleventh séance at 12.51–12.54 a.m., as at the moment that I felt the squeezes and grasps I could see both the medium's hands on the séance table ; and especially so at 1 a.m., when I alone controlled, and not only saw both Eusapia's hands, but held them separately by her thumbs in both my hands, which I kept apart on the séance table; and subsequently at 1.3 a.m., whcn I held both her thumbs in my right hand, the foot control being verified by me at the time.

It will be noted that F., as well as myself, was able to see that at 1.3 a.m. I was holding the two thumbs of Eusapia in my right hand. (I had ceased controlling, with my left hand, in order that the alleged spirit hand of my father should he better able to grasp it. Had I received a grasp in a certain manner it would have been to me a test of identity. The grasp that I received failed to give the required test.)

It is inconceivable that Eusapia should have been able to squeeze my hand and grasp my arm in this manner with one of her feet, even if she had one free, for the squeezes and grasps were clearly those of a hand. Neither could she have lifted her foot to the height of my hand and arm without a contortion of her body, which would have been immediately seen, whereas she sat quietly on her chair in a natural position. I am therefore convinced that it was neither Eusapia's hand nor her foot that squeezed and grasped me, and as I am positive that it was not the hand nor foot of any one of the sitters, I am driven to the conclusion (preposterous though it appears to me) that the supernormal force, which had given me conclusive evidence of its existence through the phenomena previously described, was able to produce the effects of tangible matter and assume the form of a hand. (The conditions under which I felt grasps and touches on other occasions at other séances than those referred to above offered me also strong evidence that the touches and grasps were independent of the physical organism of Eusapia. The numerous touches on my back between 12.11 and 12.20 in Séance X. occurred under what were to me excellent test conditions, as at the very time that I was feeling them I was constantly passing my left hand all up her left arm to her shoulder and down her left leg to her foot, thus verifying that I had undoubted control of her left hand and foot with my right hand and foot, and that the touches were not produced by her head. F. had control of her right hand and foot.)

Its is not, however, the above phenomena of touches

and grasps that I would bring forward as crucial evidence for the existence of a supernormal force, as some of the test conditions which I have specified were lacking in these cases. I would rather depend on the phenomena which took place in light when the medium's hands were distinctly seen simultaneously with her whole body down to her feet.

I refer here only to phenomena which occurred while I was personally controlling. The reader will find in the Report others of equal evidential value, during the occurrence of which the same crucial test conditions prevailed, when F. and C. controlled.

I am compelled to accept as true the first part of the third hypothesis, "that some of the phenomena were genuine" (the second part I have already dealt with) ; it follows that the fourth hypothesis, "that some of the phenomena were genuine and the others not proved to be either genuine or fraudulent," is that which represents my attitude.

In previous investigations with other so-called physical mediums, I had formed the opinion that, as I had detected them resorting to fraud in the majority of their phenomena, the other phenomena in which I did not detect fraud were presumably also fraudulent. As regards Eusapia's phenomena at these séances, my opinion is that, as some of the phenomena appear to me to be undoubtedly genuine, others in which I did not detect fraud were (considering the manner and strictness of the control and the amount of light in the séance room) also genuine. I do not maintain this of all the phenomena, as the chances of occasional mal-observation on our part, at such rare times as when darkness prevailed or when the controllers were changing their seats, cannot he excluded. At the same time I must repeat that Eusapia was not detected in fraud in any one of the 470 phenomena that took place at the eleven séances.

My general opinion of these phenomena is that they were due to some supernormal force resident in the organism of Eusapia, though some few of them would appear to point to the action of an independent energy.

Whatever explanation is advanced can only be a theoretical one. It is not theories that are required at this stage of the investigation of this medium, (who so far has only been examined by one English and a few foreign eminent men of science), but the recognition by the scientific world at large of the occurrence of supernormal phenomena. It is greatly to be regretted, in view of the reports of the eminent scientific men just referred to, that British men of science do not take the opportunity of an investigation into Eusapia Paladino's mediumship, —an opportunity which, if not taken soon, may, in nature's course, be lost, forever.

6th March, 1909

Final note by Everard Fielding

I have but little to add to the notes of my colleagues and to the Report, the length of which must have exhausted the attention of the most earnest student of the subject with which it deals. I propose to allow myself only a few words as to the character of the Report itself.

In preparing it for press I have speculated much as to what measure of success we have attained towards achieving the modest object we have had in view ; namely, to present to readers who have never assisted at séances of the kind described a complete record of the conditions which prevailed, and an accurate account of the occurrences, so that they might themselves come to a conclusion as to whether these occurrences were due to conjuring, or to a display of telekinetic force. Our intention at the outset was not to obtrude our own views, but to let the facts speak for themselves.

In both of these respects our intention has been largely modified in practice. There is no question but that the shorthand reports give in most cases an inadequate account of the proceedings by constantly understating the number of the phenomena and insufficiently recording the adequacy of the control which prevailed, with the result that a critical reader, loth to accept the hypothesis of a supernormal agency having been at work, will find the proportion of phenomena which he is able to dismiss as inconclusive, by reason of the omission from the report of some important detail, far larger than we ourselves, from our contemporary observation, could so dismiss.

It was perhaps because we so often found when reading the reports through the day after the séance, that we had fallen thus far short of our ideal in the way of reporting, and had, in a sense, done the phenomena an injustice, that we were forced from our proposed colourless attitude into one of almost proselytizing affirmation. The result is that the Report is far more positive in its conclusions and dominated by a far more personal note than, for example, the admirably balanced report recently issued by the Institute Général Psychologique of Paris, a report which, though dealing with experiments lasting through three years and marked by more remarkable incidents than any in our own experience, is nevertheless drawn up with such a wealth of scientific caution and reserve as almost to leave a reader in doubt as to the character of its own conclusions.

It has constantly, and in my opinion most absurdly,

been said that no one is so easy to deceive as a man of science. I think it would be nearer the mark to say that if in fact there be such a thing as a supernormal physical force, no one is so easily converted to a belief in it as a conjuror. The savant, steeped in his experience of the normal forces of nature, is constitutionally averse from the conception of an apparently bizarre departure from them. Aware of his own lack of knowledge of the possibilities of mere legerdemain, he naturally prefers to suspect himself of having been the sport of some undiscovered form of deception rather than to remodel his philosophy. The conjuror, on the other hand, has the experience, not only of the possibilities, but also of the limitations, of his own art, and having no particular philosophy beyond that of an ordinary layman regarding the forces of nature, has no special difficulty in remodelling it, if necessary, when confronted with a series of events which he knows his art is incapable of explaining.

My colleagues, then, having come to the deliberate opinion that a large proportion of the manifestations of which we were the witnesses in Naples were clearly beyond the possibilities of any conceivable form of conjuring, entertain no difficulty in saying so in precise terms, and so far as my own position as a layman entitles me to it, I associate myself entirely with their conclusions without apology for our seeming lack of scientific caution.

I permit myself to finish with a quotation from a paper which I read before the Society when introducing to it the subject of this Report.

"While I have convinced myself of the reality of these phenomena and of the existence of some force not yet generally recognised which is able to impress itself on matter, and to simulate or create the appearance of matter, I refrain for the present from speculating upon its nature. Yet it is just in this speculation that the whole interest of the subject lies. The force, if we are driven, as I am confident we are, to presuppose one other than mere conjuring, must either reside in the medium herself and be of the nature of an extension of human faculty beyond what is generally recognised ; or must be a force having its origin in something apparently intelligent and external to her, operating either directly from itself, or indirectly through or in conjunction with some special attribute of her organism. The phenomena then,—in themselves preposterous, futile, and lacking in any quality of the smallest ethical, religious, or spiritual value,—are nevertheless symptomatic of something which, put at its lowest by choosing the first hypothesis, must, as it filters gradually into our common knowledge, most profoundly modify the whole of our philosophy of human faculty ; but which, if that hypothesis is found insufficient, may ultimately be judged to require an interpretation involving not only that modification, but a still wider one, namely, our knowledge of the relations between mankind and an intelligent sphere external to it. Although one may approach the investigation of the phenomena themselves in a light, shall I say, even a flippant spirit—(I sometimes think that in this way alone one can preserve one's mental balance in dealing with this kind of subject),—one must regard them as the playthings of the agency which they reveal, and the more perfect revelation of that agency, whatever it may be, through the study of them, is surely a task as worthy of the most earnest consideration as any problem with which modern science is concerned.

If our report, by reason of its form and detail, is found to do something towards supplying a further evidential basis for, and therefore directing the attention of men of science in this country towards, the far more important and elaborate published invetigutions of many of our more eminent predecessors, and of inducing them to take a part in the research, I shall feel that it has amply served its purpose."

Modern Spritualism, A History and Criticism:
Eusapia Paladino
(1904)

By Frank Podmore

Eusapia Paladino has been a medium for many years, and has been the subject of experiments by several groups of observers, which have been reported at considerable length in the continental periodicals devoted to Spiritualism.

According to her own account, she was born in 1854. We read in the *Spiritual Magazine* of 1872, p. 287, of a physical medium named Sapia Padalino (no doubt a corruption of the Italian medium's name), who would write with her naked finger, leaving marks as if made with a pencil. The trick is a favourite one with Eusapia in recent times.

Her name first came prominently before the English public in 1893, as a result of the investigations conducted at Milan in the previous autumn by a group of scientific men — Professors Schiaparelli, Brofferio, Finzi, Gerosa, and others. Charles Richet and Lombroso also attended a few of the seances. The chief manifestations observed in the light were the lifting of a fairly heavy table, with the medium sitting at one end of it, her hands being held and the lower portion of her body being under observation, and an oscillation—to the extent of some 17 lbs.—in the weight indicated by the balance when Eusapia was sitting on the platform of a weighing machine, The results obtained seemed to the Committee inexplicable, but neither form of experiment succeeded when stringent precautions were taken to prevent the contact of any portion of the medium's dress, with the leg of the table in the one case, with the floor on which the balance rested in the other. The Committee expressed themselves satisfied that the results were not due to mechanical artifices, but Richet, in a separate report, arrived at a more cautious conclusion.

It is, however, primarily the phenomena observed in the dark circle with which we are now concerned — movements of furniture and other objects, raps, the appearance and touch of hands, and other manifestations of familiar types. To the Milan Committee these also seemed all but conclusive ; but Professor Richet again pointed out the weak spot in the evidence. The things would be inexplicable if we could be sure that Eusapia could not use her hands.

Professor Richet was nevertheless so impressed by his experiences that eighteen months later, in the summer of 1894, he invited a small party of friends to a series of experiments with Eusapia at his own house, on the Ile Roubaud, near Hyères. Amongst those who attended the investigation were Dr. Ochorowicz, Professor Oliver Lodge, and Mr. F.W.H. Myers. The things observed were of same general character as those recorded at Milan, and at hundreds of other séances with other physical mediums for the last fifty years ; that is, when the medium was sitting at an ordinary table, with the members of the circle ranged on each side of her and the room carefully darkened by her directions, a musical box would be wound up, small articles would be brought from distant parts of the room and placed on the table in front of the investigators, heavy pieces of furniture would occasionally be moved, the touch of hands would be felt, shadowy hands occasionally seen, and so on. Apart from the scientific distinction of the investigators, the history of these seemingly trivial performances is worthy of note (1) because a contemporary record of the whole proceedings was kept by a note-taker stationed outside the room, within hearing of all that took place ; (2) because the observers named—none of them without previous experience in such matters—professed themselves satisfied that the precautions taken to prevent Eusapia's physical participation in production of the phenomena were sufficient.

Even if the medium had the free use of her hands, Prof. Lodge and Mr. Myers, at any rate, considered that it have been difficult, if not impossible, for her without leaving her seat to have done the things that were done in their presence at the earlier sittings. At the later meetings of the series, however, the character of the phenomena, by the general testimony of the observers, appears to have deteriorated, for Mrs. H. Sidgwick, who, with the late Professor Sidgwick, attended some of these later meetings, was of opinion that all the phenomena which she witnessed could have been produced by the medium if her hands alone had been free.

In any case, the proof of the supernormal agency in which Professor Lodge and other witnesses were disposed, on the strength of these manifestations, to believe, depended primarily on the effectiveness of the means adopted to secure the medium's body and limbs. For if the medium could free a hand, or even on occasion a foot, the question whether she could by the use of those limbs overthrow a heavy table, or take out a key from a distant door, could be satisfactorily determined only by exact measurements of a kind for which in the actual conditions there was apparently no opportunity.

In Dr. Lodge's report, it appears that most of the manifestations occurred within the immediate neighbourhood of the medium, and none can be said demonstrably to have taken place outside the radius of the possible action of her hand or foot, especially if either were armed with some instrument, such as a lazy-tongs. The amount of force exerted in some feats, such as overthrowing a heavy table, was no doubt very remarkable, but not more remarkable than the extraordinary muscular power of Eusapia's left hand, as demonstrated by Dr. Lodge's dynamometer. Eusapia sent the index to 210 (indicating a force of 168 lbs.) ; none of the rest of the party at the time got beyond 152, though Dr. Lodge can, under favourable circumstances, register 170 = about 133 lbs. apparently.

Again, the writing with a bare finger (in the light) and other feats of writing markedly resemble conjuring tricks ; the lifting of a table by Eusapia standing could probably, as Dr. Hodgson pointed out and as Dr. Lodge admitted, have been effected by a simple mechanism ; the bulging of the curtain constantly observed at séances with Eusapia, taken in conjunction with the large, vague, semitransparent shadowy faces seen at other séances and the prolonged blowing of the medium *comme pour allumer du feu*, strongly suggest the employment of a collapsible bladder.

Now there is a time-honoured device, exposed in the seventies by Moncure Conway, and afterwards by Maskelyne and others, by which mediums at dark séances succeed in freeing theimelves from the control of the sitter. It may be described briefly as the art of making one hand (or one foot) do duty for two. Thus, if the hand is to be freed, the medium will contrive that one at least of her neighbours shall have control only of a part of her hand. This partial control may be of various kinds: either, as described by Richet, the medium may place her fingers, or some of them, on the hand of the sitter ; or, the sitter may be allowed to grasp two fingers only of the medium's hand ; or, as at some American séances the medium may clasp both his hands upon the bare arm of the sitter, subsequently withdrawing one and making the remaining hand, widely outspread, do duty for both.

During the séance, by a series of convulsive movements such as are commonly observed in the case of Eusapia, and indeed, in mediums generally, before the outburst of the physical manifestations, she will bring her two hands into close proximity on the table, and then, at a favourable moment, will withdraw one hand, leaving the other in contact at the same time with the hand of each of her neighbours, who will each, of course, believe that they are touching a different hand. Some device of the kind [it may be inferred from the description from Professor Richet] Eusapia had employed at the Milan investigation. The investigators of the Ile Roubaud were not ignorant of this danger. Both hands and both feet of the medium were held or controlled, the hands as a rule being held by the hands of one or more of the sitters, the feet controlled either by the hands or feet of an investigator, or by a piece of mechanism devised for the purpose. Moreover, the investigators frequently took occasion to assure themselves, before or after the occurrence of a manifestation, that the sitters detailed to guard the several parts of the medium's person were not neglecting their duty. Nevertheless, when the notes of some of the sittings reached Dr. Hodgson, he pointed out that the precautions described therein did not expressly exclude trickery of the kind indicated. Briefly, Dr. Hodgson's contention was that mere general statements to the effect that Eusapia's hands and feet were held throughout the sitting give us no assurance that a hand or a foot could not be freed for fraudulent purposes.

Effectively to guard against trickery at a dark séance it is essential that the investigators should fully realise the precise nature of the trickery to be guarded against, and should undertake and maintain throughout the séance express precautions against such trickery. That those dangers were exactly realised and those precautions continuously maintained, the report did not show ; in place of explicit descriptions of the method of holding, the notes furnish, for the most part, bare statements to the effect that Eusapia's hands, feet, and head were held by one or other of the sitters. Nor could these defects in the contemporary records be remedied by an assertion given in general terms some months afterwards of the investigators' conviction that the hands were securely held.

The next act was of a dramatic kind. Eusapia came to this country in the summer of 1895, and gave a series of sittings at Mr. Myers' house at Cambridge. At these sittings the investigators (including, at the end of the series, Dr. Hodgson himself) satisfied themselves that the medium did habitually, by devices similar to those above described, contrive to set free her hand or foot, or, on occasion, her head, and that the great bulk of the feats exhibited at Cambridge were to be explained in this way.

It may fairly be contended that the demonstration of trickery on the part of a medium, even trickery of a kind which implies long and assiduous practice, ought not seriously to prejudice the results of any investigation in which it can be shown that adequate precautions had actually been taken to guard against such trickery, for it is not antecedently improbable, on the assumption that the medium is endowed with supernormal powers, that she should occasionally cheat.

The triumph of Dr. Hodgson's demonstration lacked, it must thus be admitted, something of completeness. His argument did not, and from its nature perhaps could not, convince the investigators of the Ile Roubaud. Mr. Myers' belief was, indeed, shaken, if not actually overthrown at the time. [Later, however, as a sequel to some sittings held with Eusapia in Paris, in December, 1898, at which both Myers and Richet were present, these two gentlemen and Dr. Lodge took occasion, at a general meeting of the S. P. R., held in the following January, to reaffirm their belief in the genuineness of some at least of the physical phenomena occurring in the presence of Eusapia.] Professor Richet and his colleagues believed, on evidence which seemed to them at the time sufficient and would no doubt equally have seemed sufficient to any other investigators who had not had previous personal experience of the kind of fraud probably employed, that the precautions taken were effectual. Unfortunately the record of those precautions, as shown, is incomplete. The evidence that the holding was effective and continuous, consists, essentially, in the recollection of a series of impressions of the least intellectual of our senses. Now tactile impressions, vague, faint, and nameless at the time, present in the retrospect no picture at all comparable in precision and intensity to the memories of things actually seen.

It seems a legitimate conclusion that all the feats which could be explained on the assumption that Eusapia had free use of any limb must be left out of account. The remainder seem neither sufficiently numerous nor sufficiently striking to justify suspension of judgment. The margin of error in circumstances so little favourable to exact observation is necessarily wide, and it is scarcely unfair to assume that a proved trickster may have other tricks as yet undiscovered.

In fine, if we decide to reject the evidence in favour of Eusapia's supernormal powers, that decision is in the last analysis justified, not by the completeness of the explanation offered by Dr. Hodgson, which is necessarily based largely on conjecture, nor by the apparent lacuna in the evidence, nor, by any specific distrust of the competence of the distinguished investigators of the Ile Roubaud. The justification is that the results attained, even when vouched for by such high authority, depending, as they do, on observation, and not on automatic record, are not sufficiently free from ambiguity to weigh against the presumption derived, as from an examination of all previous evidence upon the subject. Furthermore, the presumption is strengthened, as regards these particular observations, by the reflection that other experimenters, inferior perhaps in general competence, but placed in circumstances much more favourable to observation, have been deceived again and again by devices not less obvious, when explained.

Not the least instructive feature in the history of Eusapia is the attitude of some other continental investigators who subsequently held sittings with her. In the autumn of 1895, immediately after the Cambridge fiasco, Messrs. Sabatier, de Rochas, Dariex, de Watteville, and others had a series of six sittings. They had been furnished by Mr. Myers with a full account of the manner in which Eusapia had produced fraudulent phenomcna in this country ; but they failed to profit by the lesson. Eusapia's feet were still "controlled," as a rule, by being placed on the feet of the investigator, or vice versa ; and one of her hands was still allowed to be placed on, instead of being held by, the hand of her neighbour ; the light was subdued in accordance with the medium's wishes ; and the liberality of the investigators was rewarded by an abundance of the usual manifestations. The chronicler of a still more recent series of sittings, M. de Fontenay, ostentatiously proclaims his contempt for the rediculous criticisns of Dr. Hodgson, and excuses himself from the intolerably tedious task of describing in detail the precautions taken. The reader is asked to accept his assurance that they were "more than sufficient" for their purpose.

AFTER DEATH—WHAT?
Experiments with Eusapia
(1909)

By Cesare Lombroso

THE CHIEF objection had disappeared which I had to occupying myself with spiritistic phenomena, as phenomena that could not really exist because contrary to physiological laws ; and, although the thing was still repugnant to me, I ended by accepting, in March, 1891, an invitation to be present at a spiritualistic experiment in full daylight in a Naples hotel and *tête-a-tête* with Eusapia Paladino. And when I then and there saw extremely heavy objects transferred through the air without contact, from that time on I consented to make the phenomena the subject of investigation.

Eusapia Paladino was a poor orphan girl, born at Murge in 1854, and abandoned by the roadside, so to speak. As a young girl she was received out of charity as nurse-maid in a family of the upper bourgeoisie. From the time when she was a little girl she had manifestations, either mediumistic or hallucinatory, whichever they were, without being at all able to explain them to herself, — such as hearing raps on pieces of furniture on which she was leaning, having her clothes or the bedcovers stripped from her in the night, and seeing ghosts or apparitions. In 1863 Damiani, — who at a séance in London had already heard a mediumistic communication from "John" to the effect that there was a medium in Naples, John affirming her to be his daughter, —

Damiani, I repeat, was present at a spiritualistic séance in the house of the family in which Eusapia was living. During this séance her participation in the proceedings was attended by the most extraordinary phenomena of raps, movement of objects, etc. From that time on Damiani and Chiaia got a true mediumistic eduction through her; and the poor nurse-girl, finding in this a means of gain and a method of introducing variety into her miserable occupation, went on from time to time attending seances, until the business of mediumship became her sole occupation.

The description of all the experiments made in Europe with Eusapia Paladino would fill a huge volume. We shall simply content ourselves with describing in full the seventeen seances held in Milan in 1892, with myself and with Aksakoff, Richet, Giorgio Finzi, Ermacora, Brofferio, Gerosa, Schiaparelli, and Du Prel, — seances in which the most marked precautions were taken, such as searching the medium, changing her garments, binding her and holding her hands and feet, and adjusting the electric light on the table so as to be able to turn it off and on at will.

PHENOMENA OBSERVED IN THE LIGHT

1. *Lateral Levitation of the table under the hands of the Medium seated at one of the Shorter Sides thereof.* We employed for this experiment a fir table made expressly for the purpose. Among the different movements of the table employed to indicate replies it was impossible not to note the raps frequently given by its two sides, which were lifted simultaneously under the hands of the medium without any preceding lateral oscillation. The blows

were given with force and rapidity and generally in succession, as if the table were fastened to the hands of the medium. These movements were the more remarkable in that the medium was always seated at one end of the table, and because we never once let go of her hands and feet. Inasmuch as this phenomenon appears very frequently and is produced with the greatest ease, in order that we might observe it better we left the medium alone at the table with her two hands completely above it and her sleeves turned up as far as the elbows.

We remained standing about the table, and the spaces above and below it were well lighted. Under such conditions the table rose at an angle of from 30 to 40 degrees and remained thus for some minutes, while the medium was holding her legs stretched out and striking her feet one against the other. When we then pressed with one hand upon the lifted side of the table, we experienced a marked elastic resistance.

2. *Measure of the Force applied to the lateral levitation of the Table.* For this experiment the table was suspended by one of its ends to a dynamometer attached to a cord. The cord was tied to a small beam resting on two wardrobes. Under such circumstances the end of the table was lifted 15 centimetres and the dynamometer indicated 33 kilograms. The medium sat at the same short end of the table with her hands completely above it to the right and left of the point where the dynamometer was attached. Our hands formed a chain upon the table, without pressure, and in any case they would not have been able to do more than increase the pressure applied to it. The desire was expressed that the pressure should diminish instead of increase, and soon the table began to rise on the side of the dynamometer. M. Gerosa, who was following these indications, announced the diminution as

expressed by the successive figures 3, 2, 1, 0 kilograms. In the end the levitation was so great that the dynamometer rested horizontally on the table. Then we changed the conditions, putting our hands under the table. The medium especially put hers, not under the edge where it might have touched the vertical cornice and exerted a push downward, but under the very cornice that joined the legs together, and touched this, not with the palm, but with the back of the hands. Thus all the hands could only have diminished the traction upon the dynamometer. When the wish was expressed that this traction might again increase, M. Gerosa presently announced that the figures had increased from 3.5 up to 5.6 kilograms.

During all these experiments each foot of the medium remained beneath the nearest foot of her neighbor to the right and the left.

3. *Complete levitation of the Table.* It was natural to conclude that if the table, in apparent contradiction with the law of gravitation, was able to rise on one side, it would be able to rise completely. In fact, that is what happened, and these levitations are among those of most frequent occurrence in experiments with Eusapia. They were usually produced under the following conditions: The persons seated around the table place their hands on it and form the chain there. Each hand of the medium is held by the adjacent hand of the neighbor on each side ; each of her feet is under the foot of her neighbor ; these furthermore press against her knees with theirs. As usual, she is seated at one of the short sides (end) of the table, — the position least favorable for mechanical levitation. After a few minutes the table makes a lateral movement, rises now to the right and now to the left, and finally is lifted wholly off its four feet into the air, horizontally, as

if afloat in a liquid, and ordinarily to a height of from 10 to 20 centimetres (sometimes, exceptionally, as high as 60 or 70), then falls back on all four feet at once. Sometimes it stays in the air for several seconds, and even makes fluctuating motions there, during which the position of the feet under it can be thoroughly inspected. During the levitation the right hand of the medium frequently leaves the table with that of her neighbor and remains suspended above it. Throughout the experiment the face of the medium is convulsed, her hands contract, she groans and seems to be suffering.

In order better to observe the matter in hand we gradually retired the experimenters from the table, having noticed that the chain of several persons was not at all necessary, either in this or in other phenomena. In the end we left only a single person besides the medium, and placed on her left. This person rested her feet on the two feet of Eusapia, and one of her hands on the latter's knees. With her other hand she held the left hand of the medium, whose right lay on the table in full view of all, or was even lifted into the air during the levitation.

Inasmuch as the table remained in the air for several seconds, it was possible to secure several photographs of the performance.

A little before the levitation it was observed that the folds of the skirt of Eusapia were blown out on the left side so far as to touch the neighboring leg of the table. When one of us endeavored to hinder this contact, the table was unable to rise as before, and was only enabled so to do when the observer purposely allowed the contact to occur. It will be noticed that the hand of the medium was at the same time placed on the upper surface of the table on the same side, so that the leg of the table there was under her influence, as much in the lower portion by means of the skirt as in the superior portion through the avenue of the hand. No verification was made as to the degree of pressure exerted upon the table at that moment by the hand of the medium, nor were we able to find out, owing to the brevity of the levitation, what particular part was in contact with the garment, which seemed to move wholly in a lateral direction and to support the weight of the table.

In order to avoid this contact it was proposed to have the levitation take place while the medium and her coadjutors stood on their feet, but it did not succeed. It was also proposed to place the medium at one of the longer sides of the table. But she opposed this, saying that it was impossible. So we are obliged to declare that we did not succeed in obtaining a complete levitation of the table with all four of its legs absolutely free from any contact whatever, and there is reason to fear that a similar difficulty would have been met in the levitation of the two legs that stood on the side next the medium.

4. *Variations of Pressure exerted by the Entire Body of the Medium seated upon a Balance.* This experiment was very interesting, but very difficult to perform; for it will readily be understood that every movement of the medium, whether voluntary or not, on the platform of the balance, could produce oscillations of the platform and hence of the lever, or beam. In order that the experiment might be conclusive, it was necessary that the beam of the balance, once it had taken a new position, should remain there for a few seconds to permit the measurement of the weight by means of the shifting of the weight on the beam. In the hope that this would work all right the attempt was made. The medium was seated in a chair on the balance, and the total weight was found to be 62 kilograms. After a few oscillations there was a marked

descent of the beam, lasting several seconds, and this permitted M. Gerosa, who stood near the beam, to measure the weight immediately. It indicated a diminution of pressure equivalent to 10 kilograms.

A wish having been expressed that the opposite result might be obtained, the extremity of the beam quickly rose, indicating this time a rise of io kilograms.

This experiment was repeated several times, and in five different seances. Once it gave no results, but the last time a registering apparatus enabled us to get two curves of the phenomenon. We tried to produce similar deflections ourselves, and succeeded only when many of us stood on our feet on the platform of the balance and rested our weight now on one of its sides and now on another, near the edge, with very vigorous movements, which, however, we never observed in the medium, and which, indeed, were impossible in her position on the chair. Nevertheless, recognizing that the experiment could not be regarded as absolutely satisfactory, we rounded it out with one that will be described [below].

In this experiment of the balance, also, it was noticed by some of us that success seemed to depend on contact of the garments of the medium with the floor upon which the balance was directly placed. The truth of this was established by a special experiment on the 9th of October. The medium having been seated on the balance, that one of our number who had taken upon himself to watch her feet soon saw the lower folds of her dress swelling out and projecting in such a way as to hang down from the platform of the balance. As long as the attempt was made to hinder this movement of the dress (which was certainly not produced by the feet of the medium), the levitation did not take place. But as soon as the lower extremity of the dress was allowed to touch the floor, repeated and very evident levitations took place, which were designated in very fine curves on the disc that registered the variations of weight.

5. *The Apparition of Hands on a Background slightly Luminous.* We placed upon the table a large cardboard smeared with phosphorescent material (sulphide of calcium) and placed other pieces of the same cardboard in other parts of the room. In this way we very clearly saw the dark silhouette of a hand projected on the cardboard of the table, and upon the background formed by the other pieces we saw the black outline of the hand pass and repass around us.

On the evening of September 21 one of us several times saw the apparent shadow, not of one, but of two hands, outlined against the feeble light of a window closed merely by panes of glass (outside it was night, but not completely dark). These hands were seen to be in rapid motion, but not so much so as to hinder our seeing their outlines. They were completely opaque. These apparitions (of hands) cannot be explained as cunning tricks of the medium, who could not possibly free more than one of her hands from control. The same conclusion must be drawn as to the clapping of two hands, the one against the other, which was heard several times during our experiments.

6. *The Levitation of the Medium to the Top of the Table.* Among the most important and significant of the occurrences we put this levitation. It took place twice, — that is to say, on the 28th of September and the 3rd of October. The medium, who was seated near one end of the table, was lifted up in her chair bodily, amid groans and lamentations on her part, and placed (still seated) on the table, then returned to the same position as before, with her hands continually held, her movements being accompa-

nied by the persons next her.

On the evening of the 28th of September, while her hands were being held by MM. Richet and Lombroso, she complained of hands which were grasping her under the arms ; then, while in trance, with the changed voice characteristic of this state, she said, "Now I lift my medium up on the table." After two or three seconds the chair with Eusapia in it was not violently dashed, but lifted without hitting anything, on to the top of the table, and M. Richet and I are sure that we did not even assist the levitation by our own force. After some talk in the trance state the medium announced her descent, and (M. Finzi having been substituted for me) was deposited on the floor with the same security and precision, while MM. Richet and Finzi followed the movements of her hands and body without at all assisting them, and kept asking each other questions about the position of the hands. Moreover, during the descent both gentlemen repeatedly felt a hand touch them on the head.

On the evening of October 3 the thing was repeated in quite similar circumstances, MM. Du Prel and Finzi being one on each side of Eusapia.

7. *Touchings.* Some of these are worthy of being chronicled with some detail on account of certain circumstances capable of yielding interesting bits of information as to their probable origin ; and first of all should be noticed those touchings felt by persons beyond the reach of the hands of the medium. Thus, on the evening of October 6, M. Gerosa, who was at a distance from the medium of three places (about four feet, the medium being at one short end of the table and M. Gerosa at one of the adjacent corners of the opposite end), having lifted his hand to be touched, several times felt a hand strike his to lower it ; and he, persisting, was

struck with a trumpet, which a little before had been sounded here and there in the air.

In the second place should be noted touchings that constitute delicate operations impossible to be performed in the dark with that precision which was observed in them by us. Twice (September 16 and 21) Signor Schiaparelli's spectacles were removed and placed on the table before another person. These spectacles are fastened to the ears by means of two elastic spiral springs, and it will be readily understood that a certain amount of attention is requisite in order to remove them, even in broad daylight. Yet they were removed in complete darkness with such delicacy and deftness that their owner had to touch his temples with his hand in order to assure himself that they were no longer in place.

In all of the extremely numerous maneuvers executed by mysterious hands there was never noted any blunder or collision such as is ordinarily inevitable when one is operating in the dark ; and the darkness was in most of our experiments, with one or two exceptions already indicated, as complete as it could possibly be. It may be added in this connection that bodies quite heavy and bulky, such as chairs and vessels full of clay, were placed upon the table without encountering any one of the numerous hands resting upon it, — a matter which was especially difficult in the case of chairs that would cover a large part of the table's surface owing to their size. A chair was once even turned down on the table and placed longitudinally without annoyance to any one, although it occupied nearly the whole top of the table.

8. *Contacts with a Human Face.* One of us, having expressed a desire to be kissed, felt the contact of two lips. This happened twice, September 21 and October 1. On three separate occasions it happened to one of those who

were present to touch a human face with hair and beard, and the touch of the skin was undeniably that of a living man's face. The hair was much coarser and ranker in growth than the medium's, but the beard seemed very soft and fine.

9. *Sound of a Trumpet.* On the evening of October 3, a trumpet having been placed behind the medium and behind the curtain, all at once we heard it sound several notes. Those who were near Eusapia were in a situation to assure themselves with the greatest certainty that the sound did not come from her direction.

10. *Other Instances of "Apports."* One of us, at the beginning of the séance, had laid his overcoat on a chair beyond the reach of the medium. At the close it was seen that several different objects had been brought and laid on a phosphorescent cardboard that was on the table. The owner of these articles recognized them at once as having been in an inside pocket of his overcoat. Hereupon the medium began to lament and make signs of displeasure, complaining of something that had been put about her neck and was binding her tight. We produced light and found that the overcoat was not in the place where it had been originally laid, and then, giving our attention to the medium, discovered that she had on the overcoat in question, her arms being slipped into it, one in each sleeve. During the sitting her hands and feet had been always controlled in the usual way by the two who sat next her.

PHENOMENA HITHERTO OBSERVED IN THE DARK
NOW AT LENGTH OBTAINED IN THE LIGHT, WITH THE
MEDIUM IN SIGHT

In order to attain complete conviction, it remained for us to attempt to secure important phenomena in the light. But, as darkness is very favorable to their production, we proceeded, in the sitting of October 6, as follows: In order that one part of the room might be left in darkness, it was separated from the rest by a curtain (divided in the middle), and a chair was placed for the medium before the aperture in the curtain. Her back was in the dark part, while her arms, hands, face, and feet were in the illuminated portion. Behind the curtain were placed a little chair and a small bell, about a foot and a half from Eusapia, and upon another more distant chair was placed a vessel full of moist clay.

In the illuminated part of the room we formed a circle around the table, which was placed before the medium. The room was lighted by a lantern with red glass sides.

Presently the phenomena began. We saw the inflated curtain blowing out toward us. Those who sat near the medium, on opposing their hands to the curtain, felt resistance. The chair of one of them was vigorously pulled, then five stout blows were struck on it, which signified "less light." We thereupon softened the light of the red lantern with a shade; but a little afterward we were able to remove the shade, and instead the lantern was set on our table in front of the medium. The edges *(lembi)* of the curtain where it was divided were fastened to the corners of the table, and, at the request of Eusapia, the upper parts were also folded back above her head and fastened with pins.

Then above the head of the medium something began to appear and disappear. M. Aksakoff rose, put his hand in the aperture of the curtain above the head of the medium, and announced that fingers had touched him several times; next, his hand was grasped through the curtain; finally. he felt something thrust into his hand.

It was the little chair ; he held it firmly ; then the chair was snatched away from him and fell to the floor. All present put their hands through the curtain and felt the contact of hands. In the dark background of the aperture itself, above the head of the medium, the usual firefly-like bluish gleams appeared several times. M. Schiaparelli was forcibly struck through the curtain both on the back and side. His head was covered by the curtain and drawn into the dark part, while he with his left hand kept holding all the time the right of the medium, and with his right the left hand of M. Finzi. In this position he felt himself touched by the warm bare fingers of a hand, saw the light-gleams describing curves in the air and lighting up a little the hand and the body which was carrying them. Then he took his seat again ; whereupon a hand began to appear in the aperture without being withdrawn so suddenly and in a more distinct way. M. Du Prel, without letting go of the hand of the medium, put his head into the aperture above her head and received some hard blows from several quarters and by more than one finger. The hand still showed itself between the two heads.

Du Prel resumed his place, and M. Aksakoff held a pencil up to the opening. It was grasped by the hand and did not fall to the floor. In a little while it was flung through the aperture onto the table. Once a closed fist appeared on the head of the medium. It opened slowly and showed the hand open, with the fingers spread apart.

It is impossible to state the number of times that this hand appeared and was touched by us. Suffice it to say that no doubt was any longer possible! It was actually a living human hand that we saw and touched, while at the same time the entire bust and the arms of the medium remained in sight and her hands were continuously held by her neighbors on each side.

When the sitting was over, Du Prel passed first into the darkened part of the room and called out to us that there was an imprint in the clay. In fact, we ascertained that this had been disfigured by the deep print of five fingers, which explains the fact that toward the end of the séance a piece of clay had been thrown upon the table through the aperture in the curtain. The imprint of the hand was a permanent proof that we had not been under an hallucination.

These things were repeated several times in the same way or under a form a little different on the evenings of the 9th, 13th, 15th, 17th, and 18th of October.

Although the position of the mysterious hand would not permit us to assume that it belonged to the medium, nevertheless, for greater security, on the evening of the 15th an elastic rubber band was applied to her left hand and wound around each finger separately, and thus allowed one to distinguish at any moment which of the two hands each neighboring sitter had in custody. The apparitions took place just the same, as they also did on the evening of the 17th, and finally on the 18th, although with less intensity, under the rigorous control (solemnly attested by them) of MM. Richet and Schiaparelli, each of whom gave special attention to this part of the investigation.

One evening, in full light, Schiaparelli brought a block of new writing paper and asked Eusapia to write her name. She grasped his finger and moved it over the paper as if it were a pen. She then said, "I have written." But we could find no trace of writing, and she showed us that the writing was there, but in the inside of the tablet, or block of pages. In a second trial the signature was visible on the stick that held up the window curtain at a height of more than two metres at least, and nearly four from the table.

In a last trial the name was found to be badly written on the next to the last page of the tablet of paper, and yet the leaves had not been turned over nor the tablet lifted up.

And now let us glean the most interesting cases from the memoirs of the most eminent experimenters.

At Naples, in 1895, with my eminent associates Bianchi, Tamburini, Vizioli, and Ascensi, I again tried these experiments in a room in our inn chosen expressly for the purpose. And here, in full light, we saw a great curtain which separated our room from an alcove adjoining (and which was more than three feet distant from the medium) suddenly move out toward me, envelop me, and wrap me close. Nor was I able to free myself from it except with great difficulty. A dish of flour had been put in the little alcove room, at a distance of more than four and a half feet from the medium, who, in her trance, had thought, or at any rate spoken, of sprinkling some of the flour in our faces. When light was made, it was found that the dish was bottom side up with the flour under it. This was dry, to be sure, but coagulated like gelatine. This circumstance seems to me doubly irreconcilable, — first, with the laws of chemistry, and, second, with the power of movement of the medium, who had not only been bound as to her feet, but had her hands held tight by our hands.

When the lights had been turned on, and we were all ready to go, a great wardrobe that stood in the alcove room, about six and a half feet away from us, was seen advancing slowly toward us. It seemed like a huge pachyderm that was proceeding in leisurely fashion to attack us, and looked as if pushed forward by some one.

In other successive experiments made in full light with Professor Vizioli and with De Amicis, having asked Eusapia (whose feet and hands were tightly bound and held by us) to have her "John" move a little bell that had been placed on the floor about a foot and a half from her, we more than once saw her skirts extend themselves to a point, as if forming a third foot or like a swelled-up arm. When I grasped this arm, it presented a slight resistance to me, as if it were a bladder filled with gas. And this immaterial arm (shall we call it?) finally, in full light, under our very eyes, all of a sudden seized the bell and rang it!

I shall now present some of the experiments tried at Milan and Genoa before the Society for Psychical Studies by Morselli (190&–1ço7), Marzovati, and myself, and described by Barzini in his *Mondo dei Misteri* (1907).

The medium (Eusapia) frequently performed experiments suggested by the caprice of those present. One evening we asked her to produce on our table a trumpet then on a chair in the corner of the inner cabinet; and, while we were looking at Eusapia sitting there motionless, we heard the little trumpet fall to the floor, and then for several minutes we heard it moving lightly along as if a hand were grazing it without being able to grasp it. One of the experimenters held out the interrupters (or cut-offs) of the electric light entrusted to him toward the cabinet, about six feet from Eusapia, and said, "Take them!" They were at once taken out of his hand, and several metres of the cord to which the cutoffs were attached slipped through his fingers. He pulled the cord to him forcibly and felt an elastic but strong resistance. After a brief and gentle pull he exclaimed, "Turn on the light!" and one of the lamps was lighted.

These events sometimes occur so rapidly as to take one by surprise and leave in one's mind a very legitimate doubt as to their nature ; but very frequently they are slow and labored, and reveal an intense and concentrated energy.

During the seance Professor Morselli felt his right arm grasped by a huge hand, the position of the fingers of which he could accurately distinguish. At the same time Eusapia cried out, "See!" and the green lamp was lighted and again extinguished. Now, the cut-off of this green lamp, attached to a long cord that hung from the ceiling, was all the while in the pocket of Professor Morselli, who had not perceived the entrance of a hand there. We all observed that the lamp was lighted and extinguished without the click of the cut-off being heard. While we were talking, as if to confirm our impression, the lamp set to work lighting itself and extinguishing itself in the same silent manner as before.

We ought not to forget one thing: the lighting and extinguishing of the lamp corresponded to a slight movement of the index finger of Eusapia in the hollow of my hand. This synchrony between the phenomena and the movements of the medium occurred almost always in our experiments, and it is noteworthy that in these cases the active force of the medium proceeds from the side opposite to that on which the phenomenon is verified as having taken place. For instance, if the right fist of Eusapia is contracted, the person on her left will probably feel the touch of a hand, and is often able to recognize that it is a right hand. There is here a most singular crisscross, an inversion which it may be important to authenticate, in default of anything better.

A big table weighing about 24 pounds, situated in the empty recess in front of the window, and upon which someone had laid boxes of photographic glass plates and a metronome belonging to Professor Morselli, moved forward to us, then retired. The metronome got into action and began its regular tic-tac. After a while the apparatus is closed, then resumes its action, then is closed again. Now, to set a metronome in operation and stop it is not a difficult nor a long piece of work, but it is minute, and, above all, is not an operation that metronomes are in the habit of doing of themselves.

Frequently the objects that arrive on the table of the medium are accompanied by the black curtain in such a way that it is exactly as if they were brought by persons hidden in the cabinet and who put the curtain between the objects and their hands. In another séance we saw the dynamometer, which was almost in contact with the edge of the curtain, come up on the table, move about, and disappear behind the curtain. We do not hear the light noise that would have been made in laying it up somewhere, and we remark among ourselves that one could think it were being held by some person. Whereupon, lo and behold, out of the cabinet, above the head of the medium, there steals forth a hand, holding the dynamometer as if it were showing it to us. Then the hand disappears, and after some minutes the dynamometer reappears on the table. The pointer marks a pressure of 110 kilograms. It is the pressure that would be exerted by a very robust man.

There can be no doubt but that the thought of the participants in a séance exercises a certain influence upon phenomena. It seems as if our discussions were listened to in order to get from them a suggestion for the execution of the various performances. We have only to speak of the levitation of the table, and the table rises. If we rap rhythmically on its upper surface, the raps are exactly reproduced, and often in the same spot apparently. We begin to speak of the luminous appearances which have sometimes been exhibited in Eusapia's sittings, and which we have not yet seen in this sitting, when, suddenly, behold! a light appears on the knees of the medium, disappears, and then again shows itself, this time on her head, descends along her left side, becomes more intense, and finally disappears when it reaches the hip.

In continuation, Professor Morselli gives notice that he has discovered some person behind the curtain, feels its body resting against him, and we see its arms enveloped in the curtain. Unexpectedly, Barzini pokes his head into the opening of the curtain in order to look into the cabinet. It is empty. The curtain is swelled out and its voluminous folds are empty. That which on one side seems to be the form of a human body in relief, on the other appears as a *carità* in the stuff, — a moulage, or mould. One recalls the *"homo invisibile"* of Wells.

Barzini touches with his right hand, which is free, the swelling of the curtain on the outside face, and positively encounters under the stuff the resistance of a living head. He identifies the forehead, feeling the cheeks and the nose with the palm of his hand ; and, when he touches the lips, the mouth of the thing opens and seizes his hand under the thumb. He feels distinctly the pressure of a sound set of teeth.

The carillon (or music-box), intended to make a little diversion, comes upon the table as if it had fallen from above, and, resting there entirely isolated, plays for several seconds, while we look curiously on. In shape it is like a small coffee-grinder. Being so simple and so slightly musical, this instrument requires, in order to be played, the co-operation of the two hands, — one to hold it firm, and the other to turn the crank. Its *glu-glu* has scarcely ceased when we hear the mandolin sliding along over the floor. M. Bozzano sees it come out from the cabinet and stop behind Professor Morselli, where it strums two or three times. Thence it climbs up on the table, turns upside down, and ends by depositing itself in the arms of Barzini like a baby! As we placed our hands on the strings, we felt them vibrating under the touch of the unknown force, and thus also acquired the proof of touch as to the reality of the phenomena.

We observe that the movement of the mandolin, as of all the objects transported, has a kind of orientation. In other words, the objects never move in a circle: they are subject to transference, but not to revolution. They move precisely as if they were held by a hand, — advance and retreat, move to the right or to the left, but keeping one and the same relative position. The mandolin always has the handle turned toward the medium. The chairs which take their curious walks and climb up on the table always look as if they were being dragged along by the back. Professor Morselli brought with him a little cord about sixteen inches long, and at a given moment put it on the table. It disappeared and then returned, wiggling and squirming like a dog's tail. When he expressed the wish to have knots tied in it, immediately it disappeared into the cabinet and soon after returned knotted in three places. These knots were equal, large, well made, symmetrical, and equidistant.

In a fifth sitting, in which Morselli had carefully tied Eusapia to a cot-bed, he was obliged to testify, after every instance of apparition, that she had been untied or tied in a different manner.

SPECTRAL APPEARANCES AND MATERIALISATIONS

During the first five or six years of her public career as a medium, Eusapia devoted herself more to phenomena of movement — to self-moving objects of furniture and to apports — than to spectral appearances. After the first years spectral hands began to be seen (sometimes joined to arms of various size), and, more rarely, feet. In the last few years these phantasms of arms and hands appear more frequently in the middle and at the end of the séance. Sometimes they accompanied translocation of chairs and mandolins, etc. Sometimes they appeared solely for the purpose of showing themselves — frequently being pale, diaphanous, of a pearly tint.

Bottazzi (*Nelle Regioni Inesplorate della Bialogia, 1907*) multiplied observations of this kind. For instance, he saw a black fist come clear out in front of the left-hand curtain and approach a lady, who felt herself touched on the back of the neck and on the knees. On another occasion a natural hand, the warmth and solid nature of which were felt, was placed on his arm, and then re-entered the body of Madame Paladino, as if it were a case of phantasmal prolongation. Indeed, Galeotto once distinctly saw emerge from the left side of Eusapia two identically similar arms, — one (the true one) held by the controller, and another spectral (or "fluidic"), that detached itself from her shoulder, touched the hand of the controller, and then returned to merge itself in the body of Eusapia.

These "fluidic" arms are the ones with which the mediums move objects from eight to twelve inches farther than the extremity of their own proper limbs ; furthermore, the thrusts given by them frequently produce pain just as if they were the true arms. Sometimes, in good séances, these phantom limbs are somewhat prolonged, but not farther than four and a half feet from the table.

At the end of Eusapia's séances, especially the more

successful ones, true spectral appearances occurred, though much more rarely. Among the more important of these, inasmuch as it was seen by many and was repeated, I note not only the apparition of the deceased son of Vassallo, but also the one first confessed to me personally by Morselli (however put in doubt afterwards) of his mother, who kissed him, dried his eyes, said certain words to him, then again appeared to him, caressed him, and, to prove her personal identity, lifted his hand and placed it on the right eyebrow of the medium ("It is not there," said Morselli), and then placed it on her own forehead, on which, near the eyebrow, was a little blemish. Morselli was seated at the right of Eusapia, while on the other side was Porro.

I myself had the opportunity of examining a similar apparition in Genoa in 1903. The medium (Eusapia) was in a state of semi-intoxication, so that I should have thought that nothing would be forthcoming for us. On being asked by me, before the séance opened, if she would cause a glass inkstand to move in full light, she replied, in that vulgar speech of hers, "And what makes you obstinately stuck on such trifles as that? I can do much more: I can cause you to see your mother. You ought to be thinking of that."

Prompted by that promise, after half an hour of the séance had passed by, I was seized with a very lively desire to see her promise kept. The table at once assented to my thought by means of its usual sign-movements up and down; and soon after (we were then in the semi-obscurity of a red light) I saw detach itself from the curtain a rather short figure like that of my mother, veiled, which made the complete circuit of the table until it came to me, and whispered to me words heard by many, but not by me, who am somewhat hard of hearing. At that moment Eusapa was certainly held by the hand by two persons, and her height is at least four inches greater than that of my poor mother, of whose appearance she had not the faintest idea.

I was almost beside myself with emotion and begged, her to repeat her words. She did so, saying, "*Cesar, fio mio!*" (I admit at once that this was not her habitual expression, which was, when she met me, "*mio fiol*"; but the mistakes in expression made by the apparitions of the deceased are well known, and how they borrow from the language of the psychic and of the experimenters), and, removing the veil from her face for a moment, she gave me a kiss.

After that day the shade of my mother (alas! only too truly a shadow) reappeared at least twenty times during Eusapia's séances while the medium was in trance; but her form was enveloped in the curtain of the psychic's cabinet, her head barely appearing while she would say, "My son, my treasure!" kissing my head and my lips with her lips, which seemed to me dry and ligneous like her tongue.

One of the most typical and strange instances is that which happened to Massaro, of Palermo, in the séance of November 26, 1906, at Milan. Some time previously, having evoked at a turning-table the spirit of the son recently deceased, he had received from him the promise of a materialization at Milan. Having got a hint of the séances of Eusapia, he decided to be present.

At the sitting of the 26th, Morselli having taken a place in the chain, Madame Paladino remarked quite suddenly that she perceived a young man who came from a distance, and, after being questioned, specified "from Palermo"; and afterwards said, "Portrait made in the sun." Whereupon Massaro remembered that he had in his letter-case a photograph of his son taken out of doors (in the country). At the same time he was aware of being sharply tapped on the breast at the very spot where he had that picture of his son, and felt himself kissed twice on the right cheek through the curtain that hung near him; and the kisses were followed by very arch caresses, though most delicate withal. Then all of a sudden the significant touches were repeated, but this time by a hand that insinuated itself with eager movements into the inside pocket of the coat just where the letter-case was. This it opened just at the compartment that held the portrait. During this second appearance caresses and kisses were held back at first; then he felt himself seized around the body, drawn near the curtain, and repeatedly kissed. Finally there was projected on the curtain the apparition of a head bound with a white bandage, — a head which he recognized as that of his son.

A few months before he died, Chiaia presented me with some bas-reliefs obtained (all of them) from Eusapia when in a state of trance by placing clay wrapped in a thin foki of linen on a piece of wood in a box, and this covered with a board securely weighted down by a heavy stone. Upon this the medium placed her hand, and after she had entered into the trance state cried out, "It is done!" The box was opened and there was found the hollow print either of the hand or the face of a being whose facial expression was mingled of life and death. I was not present at these sittings. But the testimony of Chiaia (a man of honorable memory) and that of an illustrious Neapolitan sculptor who took the reliefs from the moulds or imprints is my firm guaranty as to the transaction; as is also the opinion of Bistolfi, according to whom, in order to obtain in a few minutes those touches which, seen near at hand, are meaningless, but which from a distance assume a terrible and positively death-life expression, repeated trials would be necessary, and we should have to grant to the medium an extraordinary artistic ability, whereas she is without the very first elements of the art. Let us add that, since the clay is covered with a thin veil, the warp and woof of which can still be made out in the imprint, even a veteran artist could not succeed by mere pressure, and, as Bozzano notes, the hand would have to leave, not an imprint proper, but a vague channelling.

The bona fide nature of these occurrences is also proved to me from their having been repeated under the eyes of Bozzano at meetings of the *Circolo Scientifico Minerva of Genoa*, in 1901–1902, and in France under the control of Flammarion at Monfort l'Amaury, who reproduces a remarkable death-like mask, the very image of Eusapia. The same phenomena have been produced under my own eyes in Milan and Turin.

EXPERIMENTS WITH ACCURATE SCIENTIFIC INSTRUMENTS

But the great mediumistic problem cannot be solved without the assistance of those accurate instruments by the use of which we are saved from every possible error of judgment.

Morselli noted a diminution of weight in Eusapia, after the trance state, amounting to 2200 grams. Arsonval at Torigio remarked that at the moment of the levitation of the table Eusapia's weight was augmented by the weight of the table. Eusapia, like Home, can vary the weight of her body both downward and upward (i.e. in less and in greater degree), first from 62 to 52 kilograms and then rising to 72 kilograms. She can effect the same result in the case of an object placed upon the balance, although at least the hem of her draperies or her dress must touch the foot of the weighing-machine *(bascule)*.

In our experiments with Eusapia we obtained similar results. Having placed two Regnier dynamometers on the table at a distance of three feet from the medium, — asking her to exert the greatest pressure she could, — we saw the indicator go to 42 kilograms, and this of itself, in full light and during one and the same manipulation. But when she is out of the trance state Eusapia has never before been able to reach more than 36. During the performance she asserted that she saw her "John" pressing in his two hands the instrument which she in her ignorance called "the thermometer." And she kept writhing her hands, held tight by us, and trying to turn them toward the dynamometer. While this was going on, I observed that the pupil of her eye contracted and her breathing grew deeper even to the point of dyspnœa.

In February, 1907, we placed in the mediumistic cabinet a Marey cardiograph at a distance of three feet from the psychic, who had her back turned to it and her hands controlled by two of the experimenters. The cardiograph was connected with a pen running upon a cylinder smoked with lampblack. The connection was made by a tube traversing the walls of the cabinet. The writing pen was located 51 centimetres from the left lateral wall of the cabinet and about a metre and a half from the medium. Everything being ready, we begged "John" to press the button of the cardiograph.

After a few minutes we hear the noise of the pen running over the cylinder, which being revolved gives us two groups of curves that rapidly decrease. One part of the second group is intertwined with the first because we were not able in the darkness to remove the cylinder in time. The first group corresponds to about 23 seconds and the other to about 18 seconds. These tracings indicate either a proneness to exhaustion or else weak volitional energy.

The psychic, who in the normal state does not exercise any influence at a distance on the electroscope, one evening when she had just been awakened from a profoimd trance was placed by Dr. Imoda with her hands suspended ten centimetres above the electroscope. For two minutes nothing happened. Then of a sudden began the drooping of the pieces of gold leaf, which after four minutes fell rapidly. This is something that, correlated with the impression made by the medium on photographic plates wrapped up in dark paper, confirms the fact of her radio-activity in the trance state, and harmonizes with the frequent appearance of white fluctuating clouds, similar to the luminous vapor on the upper surface of the table during the séances, it being a property of the cathode rays to determine the formation of vapor when they pass through air saturated with humidity.

And now we come to the experiments of Foà and Herlitzka and Bottazzi (*Rivista d' Italia, 1907*).

Drs. Foà and Herlitzka thus write:

In order to register objectively the movements that the medium has the power of producing, we have constructed a rotating cylinder around a vertical axis. The cylinder completes one entire revolution in six hours. Around the cylinder is wrapped a sheet of white paper covered with a layer of lampblack. Upon this black surface a fixed point moves, removing the lampblack, and through the movement of the cylinder marking on the paper a white horizontal line. If the pointer moves from above downward, it designs on the paper a delicate vertical line. The pointer could be put in motion by a small electro-magnet, the Desprez register united to an accumulator and a telegraphic key. The rotating cylinder and the Desprez register are placed under a bell-glass, which is set on a stout plank. The bell-glass, the lower rim of which is stout and thick, was fixed upon the plank by means of a narrow band passing through three eye-holes formed of little ribbons sealed with sealing-wax to the board. The rim of the bell-glass served as a hold, or stop, for the band. Through three holes made in the thickness of the wooden plank, the conducting wires proceeding from the registering apparatus issued from beneath the bell-glass only to be immediately encased in glass tubes which hindered the wilful or casual contact of the wires with each other and the consequent breaking of the electric circuit. Of the wires, one went to the accumulator, the other directly to the telegraphic key, from which next in order a third wire, insulated in a glass tube, went to the other pole of the accumulator. All parts of the wire that could not be insulated by glass, at the binding-wires of the accumulator, were wrapped with insulating ribbon and covered with a ribbon band sealed with our seal. Finally, the telegraphic key itself was enclosed in a cardboard box nailed to the plank, and shut by means of two bands placed crosswise and sealed. Two little holes in the box gave passage to two glass tubes containing the conducting wires. Accumulator and key were fixed upon the same plank as the cylinder. Thus it was impossible to make a mark upon the cylinder except when the key was pressed down.

Besides this registering mechanism, we prepared some sheets of lampblacked paper in order later to secure imprints ; some photographic plates carefully folded in black paper for the purpose of putting in evidence eventual radiations that should penetrate through the opaque media ; and, lastly, a dynamometer.

We were able to prepare experiments with assured objective results.

The medium told us that she could have moved the key of our apparatus without breaking the protecting structure if this had been of cloth instead of cardboard. So, for the second sitting, we modified our apparatus, and in order not only to register the movements taking place, but also to measure their intensity, we abandoned electric registration, substituting for it the manometric method. For this purpose we connected, by means of a glass rod, a vessel full of water (and furnished with a tube aperture near the bottom) to a U-shaped manometer containing mercury. The top opening of the vessel was covered by a strong india-rubber cloth tightly bound to the receptacle itself. In this way we had an enclosed space full of liquid, at the farther extremity of which was inserted the manometer. And since upon the mercury floated a little rod furnished with a point which made tracings on the rotating cylinder, every pressure was registered and measured in an objective document.

Experience had taught us the uselessness of sealing the bell-glass, so we gave that up. But instead we took the cylinder and the manometer out of the medium's cabinet and placed them in a visible and controllable position throughout the séance. In the cabinet we placed only the glass receptacle for water, upon the rubber cloth of which the power of the medium was to be tested. This water vessel stood in a wooden box over the top of which a cloth was stretched and nailed. The rubber cloth itself was covered with a layer of lampblack.

But even our precaution of covering the apparatus with cloth was to be shown up only too well as being of no service whatever, for at a certain moment the cloth was heard to tear.

In the presence of a phantom form one of us held a photographic plate, wrapped in paper, above the head of Eusapia and felt the plate seized by a hand covered with the curtain. M. Foà grasped it with his own hand, but that of the phantasm slipped from his and struck him. The plate is changed, and the invisible hand begins another contest, during which it holds the plate fast for several seconds. At last an unexpected blow given to the plate makes it fall on the little séance table, though without breaking it.

In continuation of the game, Dr. Arullani goes up to the little table. But it advances briskly against him and pushes him back. The doctor grabs it, and a contest ensues. During the contest the table is heard to crack. The table in question is strong and made of whitewood ; height, 80 centimetres ; length, 90 ; width, 55 ; weight, 7.80 kilograms. Dr. Arullani calls for a pressure of the hand from the curtain, and the medium replies with the voice, "I will first break in pieces the table and then shake hands." Hereupon three new complete levitations of the table take place, and each time it falls back heavily on the floor, and later goes into the cabinet, all the time smashing itself up, then comes out with violent movement, thrashing around before everybody, and, its joints all apart, is finally broken to pieces, even the separate boards being broken up. Two of the legs, still united by a small strip of wood, hang poised in the air for a moment above us and then descend upon the little séance table.

The co-experimenters of Professor Mosso thus sum up the objective phenomena established and authenticated by them:

(1.) The registration of our apparatus took place while the rotating cylinder was outside of the séance cabinet in such a way that no one could approach it without being seen, while at the same time the transmitting apparatus was in a wooden box higher than the elastic cloth, or membrane, and entirely visible. One of us felt, simultaneously with the taps on the membrane, the pressure of the right hand of the medium in his left, during which time also the other hand of Madame Paladino was in that of Professor Foà. The apparatus stood on the left of Dr. Herl itzka, whose left hand held the right hand of the medium, while her right was held by the one who sat next.

(2.) The stout table went all to pieces before the eyes of all of us, untouched by any one ; the nails were pulled out and the joints and separate boards smashed. The breaking up took place, as has been said, on one side of the medium and also in front, to the left, in the midst of many of the company, and in a good state of the light.

(3.) The photographic plate, nailed under the table, passed with swift motion to its upper surface, while all present were on their feet and forming the chain, and in the best light possible, — all of us, including the medium, being at a distance from the table, which was in open space and distinctly visible on all sides. The objective records of the phenomenon were these: When the séance was over, the photographic plate was found to be on the table instead of under it, and two of the nails that had held it up were missing. Before the event occurred, Eusapia made the one of us who had nailed the glass plate under the table give her his hand to hold, while her right was at the same time held by two others of us.

(4.) The photographic plate (wrapped up in black paper) which one of us had held on the head of the medium and which for several seconds had been struggled for by what we called a hand, showed after development the dark negative imprint of four large fingers. This is evidently a case of radio-activity and not of luminosity, because the impression was made through an opaque medium. Two of the plates gave uncertain results.

Our manometer had made on the smoked paper varied markings, the highest of which correspond to a pressure of 56 millimetres of mercury. The proportions of the elastic cloth being known, that indicates that upon this cloth there had been exerted a pressure equal to about to kilograms. Upon the gutta-percha cloth covered with lampblack there was found the imprint of the cloth ; only it was partly torn.

Bottazzi *(Nelle Regioni Inesplorate della Biologia Umana, 1904),* and Galeotti at Naples, undertook on a grand scale, in experiments with Eusapia, the application of graphic registration to mediumistic phenomena. From Bottazzi I have gleaned the following accounts: — Conceive a metallic cylinder covered with a sheet of white paper that has been smoked, — a cylinder that turns continuously on its axis with a uniform motion more or less rapid. Just touching the cylinder is the point of a pen, or stylus, which at one end is fixed to a support. The style may rest in a vertical plane in the centre of which is a horizontal axis. When the style moves over that plane, the point describes on the cylinder a curved line, the arc of a circle that has for its centre the axis around which the style moves. The style should be held by means of a counterweight in a fixed horizontal position. Upon the surface of the séance-table let there be a telegraphic key, and let the button of the key be connected with the style by means of a cotton or silk thread. Then say to the medium, "Press down the button without touching it with your visible hand, but solely by means of your mediumistic force." The medium presses it down. The click of the key is heard, that is to say, the rap of the metallic point of the key upon the metal block underneath. But at the same time, through the operation of the thread, the lowering of the button has drawn down the style, the point of which has traced a line on the smoked paper.

The telegraphic key was set in motion several times. It was screwed down on a piece of board, and hence was not misplaced or overturned. We all heard the rapid lively taps of characteristic timbre. And as a proof that we were not the victims of collective illusion or hallucination, the tracing revealed to us three groups of registrations and two isolated strokes intercalated among them. Fortunately, the electro-magnetic signal operates in a mode quite different from that of our sense organs and is never deceived, nor can be deceived. Those little vertical lines, that are almost indistinguishable one from the other (because, owing to the low velocity of the cylinder, they succeed each other at too short intervals, less than the fifth of a second), correspond to an up and down movement of the key. Looking sharply at the original tracings with a magnifying lens, one discovers that the marks when they are thick are registered with a frequency of about 2 for every of a second, that is to say, about 13 to a second.

Here is another method of manometric registration: You are to suppose fastened upon the top of a stool a

Marcy receiving tympanum, upon the central button of which, glued to the middle of the sheet of caoutchouc (more resistant than the sheets ordinarily used in physiological researches), had been fastened with strong glue a disk of wood for the purpose of increasing the superficies upon which the pressure of the invisible hand of the medium was to be exerted. The tympanum was connected by means of a tube with a François Frank mercury manometer, which, in a branch of the U-shaped tube, has a float furnished with a style that writes on the usual lampblacked cylinder. Every pressure exerted on the little wooden disk glued on to the elastic membrane is transformed (by transference of force) into a lifting of the float and of the style of the manometer, and every depression into a lowering thereof.

Now, if the tracing be observed, groups of ascending and descending white lines will be found, some higher, some lower. Naturally, to the higher lines correspond strong pressures, to the medium ones pressures of medium intensity, and to the lowest ones weak touches of the disk. The pressures given, especially the strongest, cannot produce the highest lines except when they are exerted on the membrane of the tympanum, which, as has been said, is fastened upon the stool.

As respects displacements of this stool, or as respects the taps rapped on it, or the movements imparted to the caoutchouc tube connecting the tympanum and the manometer, or even as regards the bruises or batterings of it, the former do not have any effect at all, and the latter are translated into little vertical lines on the manometric tracing. An invisible hand or foot would have to strike or step on the little disk, would have to press on the membrane of the receiving tympanum and that with force, since to obtain the highest lines it is necessary to depress the disk to the utmost limit.

In other séances Bottazzi (see his *Nelle Regioni Inesplorate*, etc.) places on the table of the medium a letter weigher (balance scales) and the lampblacked cylinder, and adjusts the style against the paper. Madame Paladino is asked to lower the little tray of the balance without touching it. The cylinder is put in motion, and the point traces on it a horizontal line during several successive turns. Some seconds pass, when, lo! the left-hand curtain is seen to advance resolutely toward the table (as if pushed by a hand hidden behind it, whose fingers are plainly seen in relief), take hold of the tray of the balance, forcibly depress it, then draw back and disappear.

We stop the cylinder [*says Bottazzi*], and all testify to the fact that the point has traced (badly, to be sure, because the invisible hand made the balance oscillate) a vertical line upon the smoked paper. Eusapia's hands were in our custody.

The next day [*continues Bottazzi*] I wanted to see how much the index of the letter balance registered when the little tray was depressed as far as in the experiment of the day before, and found that the pressure exerted on the tray must have been equivalent to 370 grams.

On the table of the medium, in these Bottazzi experiments, were the following objects: a cage of iron wire with a key inside of it ; two Erlenmayer goblets containing the two known solutions of ferrocyanide of potassium and chloride of iron ; one or two spring-keys ; and a little Gaiffe electro-magnetic mechanism suitable for use as an electric cut-off, or interrupter. The other spring-key (the mate of that just spoken of) was outside of the cabinet on a chair.

In the séance we are about to describe, the two keys

operate marvellously well. Eusapia had at length learned to follow synchronous movements to perfection.

Scarcely had the invisible hand begun to cause taps on the interior key to be heard when Bottazzi put the other key on the table and invited Eusapia to strike them both at the same time.

The tracings show different groupings of synchronous taps. The number of the taps is not always the same in the two corresponding groups. But that comes from the circumstance that in each group the taps begin first on the interior key or first on the exterior one, and then the taps of the other key take place. But the synchronism is always perfect. The taps present a different record on the tracing and different from that perceived by our ears. As to this, the first thing to be considered is that the mediumistic raps are rapid and shorter, while those made by the visible hand of Eusapia are more gentle and hence more prolonged. The second point respects the force with which they were made, the criterion being the intensity of the sensations they provoke in us. Now the ones exterior to the curtain were quite weak, hardly audible; the interior ones were very strong, and appeared, not simply taps, but blows of a fist bestowed on the button of the key, delivered leisurely, not forcibly driven into the two surfaces of the table.

The results obtained may he summed up thus:

The heavy table in the cabinet was shaken violently many times, with visible effort on the part of the medium, who made use of her arms and legs in such efforts. It was also from time to time drawn forth by bounds and leaps from the cabinet by the anterior left-hand corner, corresponding to the right side of Madame Paladino, and lifted up in such a way that after the sitting it was found twisted around, from front to rear and from left to right, about ten degrees measured on the level of the floor. Very naturally all the objects on it were, for this reason, either displaced or overturned (some one way, some another). Only the cylinder and the balance had preserved their original position. From the tracings we found on the smoked paper it follows that the cylinder had rotated from right to left, that is, in the direction opposite to the hands of a watch, and that the pointer of the letter weigher had traced very irregular marks, corresponding to the raps of the metallic clock upon the support of the letter balance, — sounds that we heard during the movements of the table.

Biographical Sketch of Eusapia Paladino (1907)

"AMONGST THE REVIEWS"
from
The Annals of Psychical Science

We are not concerned now with the Eusapia of dark mediumistic cabinets, amidst the sobbing and whispering, the mystery of hands, of dancing tables, of resounding raps; but the Eusapia of daylight, who, free from the paternal shade of "John," returns to her normal personality as an ordinary and altogether uneducated woman of the very lowest Neapolitan populace.

"During the two months passed by Eusapia at Turin I often saw her," writes Mme. [Paola] Carrara, "and I always thought that her real personality is as interesting as her personality as a medium, and that it is the result of the strangest product which the human race can supply.

"Eusapia is a mixture of many contrasts. She is a mixture of silliness and maliciousness, of intelligence and ignorance, of strange conditions of existence. Think of a saleswoman of Naples transplanted without any preparation into the most elegant drawlng rooms of the aristocracy of Europe. She has gained a smattering of cosmopolitan intellectuality but she has also ingenuously remained a woman of the lower class.

"She has been carried on the wing of universal renown and yet she has never cast off the swaddling clothes of illiteracy. No doubt Eusapia's illiteracy saves her from vanity, for she knqws nothing of all the rivers of ink which have been spent upon her...

"Here are a few details sufficiently piquant to awaken public interest.

"Her appearance and words seem to be quite genuine and sincere. She has not the manner of one who either poses or tricks or deceives others. Shc has had the perversity, a rare occurrence, to remain as nature made her: outspoken, sincere, instinctive, to such a degree, that however wonderful may be the tales she tells they are true.

"Her physiognomy is not ugly, although M. Barzini has discreetly insinuated that it it so. Her face is large, marked by some suffering, and bears traces rather of the spiritistic seances, of the effort and the fatigue which they involve, than of the fifty-three years that she has lived.

"She cherishes her appearance, or, at least, she shows some coquetry about it. She has magnificent black eyes, mobile and even diabolical in expression. She displays coquettishly her famous white lock among her dark hairs.

" 'Formerly,' she says, 'I was ashamed of it, but now that everyone compliments me on it 1 do not hide it any more.'

"Her hands are pretty, her feet small. She always keeps them visible outside her dress to show that they are closely shod in polished shoes."

The first time that she saw her at her father's house, Mile. Paola Carrara could not draw from her any confidences concerning her life as a medium. Instead, she told her of the feelings she had when frequenting high class society. Her impudence and arrogance as a Neapolitan of the lower class sometimes almost takes the form of personal dignity.

On one occasion, she related that she was staying with the Grand Duke in Saint Petersburg; the Grand Duchess often sent for her to come and talk to her or keep her company in the drawing-room, but when visitors came she made an imperious sign, showing her the door. Twice Eusapia rather reluctantly obeyed, but at last she rebelled and planting herself in front of the princess she said: "Madame la Grande Duchesse, you doubtless must take me for a basket which is carried to market when it is required and left in a corner when it is done with. Either I shall remain in the drawing-room with all the visitors, or I shall leave the castle." And the princess by blood, not to discontent the princess of spiritism, consented that she should remain in the drawing-room.

At Turin the Duke of the Abruzzi asked and obtained a séance with her and afterwards paid her lavishly, but Eusapia was dissatisfied. "What is a five hundred franc note to me? I am capable of tearing your five hundred franc note into four pieces" (she made a gesture of tearing it, but did not really do so), "but I do what I choose, and I choose to be treated politely." She had been very annoyed because the prince had not sent her his card.

But one day Eusapia, who ordinarily replies apathetically to those who interrogate her on this question consented to relate how she became a medium. "My history is long and incredible," she said, "but I wish to tell it to you, because everybody pretends to know it (I mean journalists), and they know nothing, and have only accumulated a heap of lies about me."

She told us that she was born at Minervo-Murge, a mountain village near Bari (Apulia). Her mother died shortly after her birth, and her father, who was a peasant, caused her to be brought up on a neighbouring farm.

But the villagers took little care of the orphan. Once when she was only a year old, she was allowed to fall, so that a hole was made in her head. That is the famous cranial opening from which, in moments of trance, a cold breeze is felt to issue. On this scar has grown a tress of hair that has always been white since infancy, and which is easily distinguishable in her photographs.

"As if I had not had trouble enough," she said, "when I was twelve years old my father died. I was thus completely alone, for I had no near relations. A native of my village, who lived in Naples, having learned my sad history, took charge of me. At Naples he put me in the care of some foreigners who wished to adopt a little girl. But I was not at all the sort they wanted, for I was like a wild animal, a forest bird, ignorant, and having always lived as a poor creature, and these ladies wanted to make of me an educated and learned girl. They wanted me to take a bath every day, and comb my hair every day, and to use a fork at table, to study French and the piano, and to learn to read and write. In fact, I was to fill up all my time with occupation and I could not amuse myself. Then began scoldings and revolt. They told me I was lazy, and, in short, in less than a year I was turned out of their house.

"I was in despair; I went again in search of that family in my own country, who gave me shelter for a few days, whilst arrangements were being made to put me into a convent. I had been in the house for a few days when, one evening, some friends came who spoke of tables that dance and give raps, things which were much talked about at that time. And, as a joke, they proposed to try and make a table turn.

"They fetched one, sat round it and called me to

come and make a chain with them. We had not sat down for ten minutes before the table began to rise, the chairs began to dance, the curtains to swell, the glasses and bottles to walk about and the bells to ring in such a fashion that all were frightened, as if in fun they had called up the devil and expected him to appear every minute. We were tested one by one to see who produced these phenomena, and they finally concluded that it was I. They then proclaimed me to be a medium and talked to everybody about it, inviting their friends and acquaintances to little spiritistic séances. They made me sit whole evenings at the table, but that was tedious to me, and I only did it because it was a way of recompensing my hosts, whose desire to keep me with them prevented their placing me in the convent. I took up laundress work, thinking I might render myself independent and live ao I liked without troubling about spiritistic séances."

"But," she was asked, "how did 'John King' [her "control"] appear on the scene?"

"That is the strangest part of my story, which many persons will not believe. At the time when I began to hold spiritistic séances in Naples, an English lady came there who had married a Neapolitan, a certain Damiani, a brother of the deputy, who still lives. This lady was devoted to spiritism. One day when she was at the table, a message came to her informing her that there was in Naples a person who had lately arrived who lived at such a number, in such a street, and was called Eusapia, that she was a powerful medium, and that the spirit who sent this message, John King, was disposed to incarnate himself in her and to manifest by marvelous phenomena. The spirit did not speak in vain, for the lady at once sought to verify the message. She went directly to the street and the number indicated, mounted to the third floor, knocked at the door and enquired if a certain Eusapia did not live there. She found me, though I had never imagined that any such John had lived either in this world or another. But almost as soon as I sat at the table John King manifested and has never left me since. Yes! I swear" (and she said this emphatically) "that all that I am telling you is the simple truth, although many persons seem to think I have arranged the facts."

Mme. Paola Carrara then relates the following anecdote, told by Eusapla Paladino:

This happened ten years ago. Eusapia says she possessed diamond ear-rings and bracelets set with emeralds, massive chains and rings with precious stones. Her rich acquaintances Sardou, Aksakoff, Richet, Ochorowicz, Semiraski, Flammarion, knowing her Neapolitn taste for gold ornaments, had loaded her with many gifts. For better security she put these treasures into a sort of strong box in her shop.

"One night," she said, "I had a horrible dream. I saw a man, of whom I saw not only the face, but all the details of his clothes; with an old hat, a handkerchief round his neck, check trousers; he came into the shop and forced open the box, whilst two companions watched at the door." The impression was so strong that she awoke her husband and told him that the shop was being robbed. He paid no attention; but she got up about two o'clock, went into the shop and asssured herself that there were no thieves there. But to set her mind at rest, she took her precious jewels and carried them to her room, where she shut them up in a piece of furniture after counting them one by one. What was her alarm next day when she encountered, near the door of the house, an individual identical in appearance with the person she had dreamed of! Worried by this thought, she went to consult a police functionary whom she knew, but he excused himself, saying: "I cannot, dear Madam, undertake to act as policeman of dreams; but if you wish to make your mind easy, take your jewels to the bank, where they will be better looked after than by my officers."

Following this sound and simple advice, she took her precious box to the bank, but she arrived too late, the doors were closed; being still uneasy, she returned to the officer and asked him to station two of his men at her door for one night. This was done. The two guards remained there all night. And on that night the dream of the theft was repeated, so that on awaking her first thought was to assure herself whether her small treasure was still in the place where she bad put it.

At about ten o'clock she went out to the shop, a few yards away from bcr house. When she reached it she bethought herself suddenly that she had been unwise to leave her jewels in the house. She returned quickly to fetch them. The entrance door was closed; but she had scarcely reached the cupboard before she perceived that the precious box had disappeared. She rushed out crying, like one possessed: "Holy Virgin, holy Virgin! my jewels are stolen. Catch the thief! catch the thief!" for she had not been out of the house ten minutes, and the thief could not be far away.

The police commissary recognised the individual, whom Eusapia described, as one of the best known theives of a gang in Naples. Afterwards Eusapia found out how he, in league with one of her servants, had succeeded in getting a false key made to fit the lock of the jewel box. "You see," Eusapia bitterly remarked, "you see what little use there is in this fine mediumistic faculty! It did not serve to save my jewels, those jewels which were dear to me as thr apple of my eye. What is to happen, happens in spite of everything!"

On being asked whether the spirits, or at least the mediumistic faculty, had intervened previously, in other circumstances of her life, she replied:

"No, I never perceive the presence of a spirit, but sometime without my being aware of it or wishing it, a spirit must have helped me. Two years ago I was ill in Paris, and I had a lazy and negligent nurse who, instead of giving me medicine, lay down on her bed and slept profoundly. I might call and ring, nobody answered. And what happened then? The lazy woman was aroused by blows and pinches which I had no intention of making, so that the nurse became alarmed by this strange phenomenon and would have nothing more to do with me and my sorceries."

Everyone who has observed and studied Eusapia, has noticed that her hands and her fingers produce a repercussion on objects and persons at a distance. The movements which her hands made in her imagination were probably movements of irritation against the nurse and resulted probably in those pinches which the nurse actually felt.

Mme. Paola Carrara thus terminates her interesting study:

"There are singular things in this nature, which seems so simple and open: certain attempts at cheating have been remarked. An observer who held more than thirty séances with her, and who saw produced by day and in full light really marvelous phenomena, asserts that two or three times in the course of the séance, she had recourse to trickery, to fraud and deceit, but so clumsily that she was easily discovered. It is not because at these moments the mediumistic faculty fails, for when controlled, she immediately afterwards produced indisputable phenomena."

On the subject of this incident of the theft of Eusapia's jewels it will interest our readers to see a letter written recently by M. François Graus to his friend M. Vincent Cavalli, which was published by *Luce e Ombra*, Milan (April, 1907). It will be observed that whilst this fresh recital contains complementary circumstances of a remarkable kind, connected with this adventure, it is not in disagreement with the narrative as given by the medium to Mme. Paola Carrara, except in one detail, that the accomplice of the theft was not a servant but Eusapia's concierge.

M. Graus also gives us a striking and humorous picture of Eusapia's consternation when she recognised that the jewels had been stolen. She was particularly indignant with John King, who could not, or would not, recover the lost objects from the thief and restore them to their owner. Every day she repaired to the police station, claiming that the thief should be caught and the objects found; but finding that time passed on and that, although a police functionary who already knew her interested himself on her behalf, nothing happened, not only did she become incapable of giving séances but she even stopped working, and spent days in weeping and talking to her neighbours of the great misfortune that had befallen her.

"Mme. Paladino knew me," continues M. Graus, "I had made many experiments with her, and she had also been present several times at some lectures of a theoretical and practical kind on animal magnetism and hypnotism, which I gave privately, about the year 1890, to some medical students.

"For these experiments I employed a subject, called

Anna del Piano, who by practice had become an excellent somnambulist.

"Eusapia thought that Mlle. del Piano might reveal the thieves to her, amd, knowing that she was not a professional, and that she did not allow herself to be put to sleep except by mc, she begged me to induce her to have a hypnotic séance for her with the object of finding the thieves.

"I at first refused, not being able to give blind credence to the oracles of somnambulism which, by suggestion or auto-suggestion, might indicate as authors of the theft persons who really were not so. But Eusapia begged so hard and wept so profusely that at last I acceded; determining that if the replies did not seem to me to justify it, I should not follow up the experiment.

"The following day, I went with Mlle. Del Piano to Mme. Paladino's house and I allowed no one else to be present at the séance. I placed Mlle. Del Piano in the somnambulistic state, and when I observed that she became clairevoyant, I commanded her to see, if possible, retrospectively, how the scene of the theft occurred and to describe it.

"I was much surprised when the somnambulist, after a few moments of concentration and after a short inspection made by turning her head with her eyes shut, all round the one room, which with one little vestibule forms Mme. Euapia'e entire lodging, began to speak and to describe the whole scene of the robbery with so many precise details concerning the persons who had participated in it, concerning their clothes and concerning the things which they had stolen from a drawer of the chest of drawers, from a cupboard in the wall and from another place, which was confirmed by Eusapia as far as she knew; the somnambulist concluded with these words addressed to Eusapia: 'Now if we go and hunt under the pillows of the concierge of your house we shall find there still a few of the objects which have been stolen.' Obviously we could not do that; the séances closed, and we left.

"The following day Eusapia returned to me and told me that she had related all this to the police inspector, of Monte Calvarfo, M. L—, who had expressed a keen desire to be present at one of these séances, and she begged me to allow him to come.

"At first I refused, but again I ended by yielding to her entreaties, and I made an appointment for a hypnotic séance to be held the following evening at Mlle. Del Piano's house; making the condition that no one should be present except Eusapia and the Inspector.

"The séance took place on the appointed day, in Mlle. Del Piano's little drawing-room, in the middle of which was a table; the room was strongly lighted by a petroleum lamp. We sat at the four sides of the table, without any intention of using it experimentally, since our object was only to put Mlle. Del Piano in the somnambulistic state, in order that she might repeat what she had said at Mme. Paladino's house, on the subject of the theft. The somnambulist repeated word for word all that she had already said, after which I awoke her.

"We then entered into conversation and I asked the inspector of police whether his suspicions concerning the authors of the theft corresponded with what the somnambulist had just said; he replied in the affirmative.

"Eusapia then spoke, and told us how after the seance held in her house she had not been able to forbear upbraiding the concierge for being in league with thieves, she and her son.

"The police inspector became very angry at this,

blaming Eusapia for the stupidity and imprudence of what she had done, which would put the thieves on the watch; he threatened to have nothing more to do with the afflair. Mme. Paladino was so affected by the just reproaches of the inspector that she fainted.

"Whilst we were helping her we noticed that the table advanced towards us, rapping repeatedly to draw our attention; and when we were all attending to it, the table signaled, by the typtological method habitual in spiritist séances, these words: 'Save my daughter, she is mad.'

"I asked how I was to do that, and the table replied: 'Give her a suggestion.'

"I remarked that the intelligence which thus spontaneously manifested could, if it chose, do that better than I; I had scarcely concluded when in full light, a phenomenon occurred which I shall never forget.

"On my left, in the space separating me from Mme. Paladino, appeared the form of an old man, tall, rather thin, with an abundant beard, who, without speaking, laid the full palm of his right hand on my head, which he squeezed between his fingers as if to draw from it some vital fluid, and when be saw fit he raised his hand and spread over Eusapia's head the fluid that he had withdrawn from my brain. He repeated this operation three times in succession, then the figure dissolved.

"Mme. Paladino immediately returned to her normal state, and from that time she never spoke again of the theft from which she had suffered, except as a bad dream. After what had occurred I remained for three consecutive days in such a condition of cerebral prostration, on account of the fluid that bad been withdrawn from me, that I could not carry on the smallest intellectual work."

FRANCESCO GRAUS.

In reply to questions that we were allowed to put to him on this subject, M. Vincent Cavalli, who is a distinguished spiritist writer, replied that his esteemed friend, Chevalier Francesco Graus, is an engineer who lives in his hotel in Rue Cavone at Naples; he is a pensioner of a large public department to which he belonged for many years. He has always been interested in magnetism and occult sciences, without, however, associating himself with any particular school. He does not lack the critical sense, as is proved, for example, by the pamphlet, *Contribution à l'étude de la Psychographie,* published by him twelve years ago, in which he studied the mediumship of Alexandra Frezza di San Felice. He does not feel at liberty to give the name of the inspector; he mentioned, however, that he was as much a believer in spiritism as himself; but, after the lapse of so many years, M. Graus cannot affirm that this functionary recognised in this occurrence the phantom of John; Mlle. Del Piano saw him clearly, and confirmed the account of this incident, which was read to her by M. Graus. The latter also remembers having talked for a long time with the constable about the apparition.

The American Séances of 1909

NEWSPAPER ACCOUNTS

from
THE NEW YORK WORLD

PALADINO IN PRIVATE SÉANCE PUZZLES EXPERTS

NEWSPAPER MAN AND MAGICIAN WITNESS WONDERFUL DEMONSTRATIONS BY THE SO-CALLED MEDIUM, BUT FAIL TO DETECT THE SOURCES OF MYSTERIOUS PHENOMENA

"Is Eusapia Paladino a marvelous psychic? Is she a clever fraud? Has she remarkable mediumistic powers? Is she a cunning trickster?

"To give its readers a chance to judge her for themselves, THE WORLD arranged a séance on different lines from any that have been held. The observers were newspaper men, trained to observe closely, to examine keenly, to describe what they saw dispassionately.

"As a precaution against feats of legerdemain there was present Howard Thurston, one of the cleverest and best informed of present-day magicians. Thurston himself performs levitation of tables and persons. He can duplicate all the ordinary spirit tricks. He knows how tables are lifted and raps are made and ghosts are raised.

"Every opportunity was given to Thurston and to the other observers to examine everything. Before the séance Madame Paladino removed all her clothing, in the presence of two women in the party, to prove that no mechanical contrivances were used.

"THE WORLD does not attempt to answer the riddle of Paladino's powers. It presents what trained observers saw. It points out where possibilities for fraud existed. With equal impartiality it details remarkable phenomena in which no evidence of trickery was manifested."

NEWSPAPER MAN FAILS TO DETECT TRICKERY IN VARIED PHENOMENA

by
William Johnston

I did not believe in spirit manifestations before witnessing the Paladino séance. I do not believe in spirit manifestations even now.

And yet:

With the little, thick-set Neapolitan woman sitting on a chair, her feet tied together and to chair legs, with myself holding firmly her right hand and foot, with a man whom I have known for many years, and have the utmost confidence in, holding the other arm and foot, with no apparent possibility of ot oppoitunitv for collusion or aid from a confederate, with properties so ordinary as to preclude the possibility of mechanical tricks, 1 saw and felt and heard many marvelous things.

I saw a plain pine table, weighing perhaps ten pounds, rise in the air eighteen inches and remain suspended by invisible forces eight or ten seconds. I saw this not once, but several times, not in darkness but in the full glare of an unshaded electric light.

I saw a little toy piano picked up from the floor and hurled down on the table before me, where with no one touching it— with no one having touched it—it sounded several notes and moved about and rocked and tilted.

I saw a child's chair, of ordinary bent wood, picked up by an invisible hand, brandished in my face and flung to the floor.

I saw black curtains hung across a corner of the room blown outward with a breeze far stronger than any one person—yes, than any ten persons—could possibly have made with their lungs.

I saw a strange rectangular shape or shadow thrust itself out from behind the curtain again and again.

I saw a luminous, slender hand drag the curtains across the table. I saw it pass up and over the body of the man opposite me. I saw it again resting on the top of Paladino's head.

I heard vibrant raps that came apparently from the under side of the table in about the center, with Paladino all the while held so tightly that movement on her part seemed impossible.

I felt a cool breeze, at least ten degrees below the temperature of the room, blowing from behind the curtains.

I felt myself slapped on the back with force, as if by someone's hand, but there was no hand there.

I felt myself slapped lightly on the cheek three times, but I could see nothing there, although it was light enough for me to see Paladino's face.

These things I know that I saw and felt and heard. Now I am not overcredulous. I have attended many séances and have seen many mediums and have seen them exposed. I have seen spirits materialized—and arrested, am familiar with the methods of misdirection and the patter to divert the attention resorted to by both mediums and magicians. I am aware, too, that Paladino has been caught in trickery. I myself have seen her levitate a table where I am positive she did it with her toe concealed beneath her gown; yet in this séance, if these strange things were done by trickery, the trickster remained uncaught.

Beginning of the Séance

The séance took place in the five-room flat of the sister of the husband of Madame Paladino, on One Hundred and Thirteen Street; Doctor Vecchio, who knew Paladino in Naples, with his wife and two or three other neighbors, Frank L. Frugone, proprietor of the ITALIAN EVENING BULLETIN, and Messrs. Paganini and Donato, from the same paper, and the wives of two of the observers, were also present.

Black muslin was tacked on the walls of a corner of the dining room. Two black curtains that reached from floor to ceiling were hung upon a cord, leaving a triangular space of a depth of two feet to the widest point.

Thurston examined the curtains for possible pockets and tapped the walls to make sure there were no secret entrances. Both Thurston and I got behind the curtains and by blowing could move them at best about six inches.

Paladino sat in an ordinary cane-seated chair in front of the cabinet. Doctor Vecchio tied her feet together and tied the cords to the feet of two other chairs, leaving about ten inches of slack. Paladino offered to have the knots sealed, but it was deemed unnecessary.

The little pine table she uses was put in front of her. Frugone on one side held her hand. Her left foot rested on his foot.

I sat on her right, with her right foot on mine, her

right hand held in mine. I kept my left hand free to test the movement of her feet. At the table besides were Thurston, Paganini, and one of the women.

Table Levitation

We formed the circle with our finger tips touching. Above our heads burned a sixteen-candle-power electric light. The table began to rock and tilt. It seemed as if some force under it was pressing it up. Several observers knocked on the table. Each time came answering knocks. The wood in the center of the table vibrated, yet it was a physical impossibility for Paladino to have struck it there. We were holding her tightly.

She lifted her hands from the table and clenched them six inches above it. She seemed to be undergoing mental strain. The table rose slowly, steadily until it was eighteen inches from the floor. There was nothing under the legs lifting it. Paladino was not touching it. After several seconds it dropped back to the floor. This took place half a dozen times.

Paladino called for less light. Someone lit the gas and extinguished the electric light. Doctor Vecchio started to turn the gas down and—apparently by accident—turned it out. For perhaps ten seconds there was total darkness until he relighted the gas. Thurston sprang behind the curtain to see if a confederate entered surreptitiously in the instant of darkness. He explored thoroughly. There was no one there. As he emerged a spirit hand seemed to seize the curtains and flung them across the table. Paladino at the same time was held hand and foot.

The next ten minutes were filled with weird manifestations. A strong, cool breeze blew from behind the curtains. Uncanny shapes thrust themselves out from the curtains in the semi-darkness. Paladino seemed in a sort of trance. Some one struck a match to light a cigarette. With an unearthly shriek she wrenched her hands from our grasp and placed them before her eyes. The light was extinguished and she subsided.

The Phosphorescent Hand

I felt a slap as from a hand on my back and turned quickly to look. There was nothing there.

I saw a slender, luminous hand emerge from behind the curtain—it looked like a woman's hand covered with phosphorus—and pass along Frugone's body. It seemed to rest for a second against his cheek. He cried out that he had been tapped on the cheek. An instant later I felt three distinct taps on my own cheek. It was light enough for me to see Paladino, to see Frugone's face across the table, and yet I could not see what had tapped me.

A little toy piano had been placed behind the curtain, it was picked up and flung down on the table before me. It rocked and tilted and something struck three or four notes on it. What it was I do not know. I only know that it was not Paladino.

The curtains twitched arid heaved. The cool breeze kept blowing. The luminous hand appeared here and there, now dragging out the curtains fully three and a half feet across the table, now resting on Paladino's head.

The child's chair that was in the cabinet was picked up and brandished in my face. I was holding one of Paladino's hands. I could see Frugone holding the other.

Paladino began to shriek and writhe like a mad person. Her hand clutched mine in a deathlike grip.

The American Séances

Paladino Unconscious

"Enough," cried Dr. Vecchio, "the séance must stop."

The electric light was turned on and Paladino covered her eyes. Thurston and I both watched the cabinet, looking for a possible confederate to emerge, but saw nothing.

The light was extinguished and a lighted candle brought in. Paladino lay back in her chair panting, unconscious, her hands still clutching ours. Her pulse was going at a terrific rate. Her face was lined with weariness. For perhaps ten minutes the doctor worked over her, and half an hour later she was still hardly herself. There was every evidence that she had gone through some sort of nerve-racking, body-tiring experience.

Frugone, Thurston, and I compared notes. To these three things we were all agreed:

—The table was levitated eighteen inches and held there without Paladino touching it.

—It was a physical impossibility for Paladino to have moved the curtains, picked up the piano, brandished the chair, and operated the luminous hand.

—There was no evidence and there seemed to be no possibility of a confederate having been concealed behind the curtains of the cabinet.

Magician Found No Confederate

by
Howard Thurston, Magician

In describing the séance I saw last Monday night, it is evident that my testimony must be accepted with the following reservation: I, myself, did not control the medium.

The controller on the left was an Italian journalist, and on the right sat Mr. Johnston of the New York World. These two maintained strict watch over the medium's hands and feet throughout the sitting.

Before we commenced, her feet were tied to the rungs of the chairs of her controllers, about ten inches of rope being allowed, so that she could not move her feet backward far enough to produce the cabinet phenomena which followed. Our first phenome na consisted of those remarkable table levitations, of which the public has already heard.

I repeatedly saw the table raised in the air a foot or more, all four feet being on the ground, her hands raised above the table, or at times barely touching the iop. The room was well-lighted and the controllers could plainly see hcr feet, and they testified that they had her hands and feet securely held during these levitations.

Variety of Manifestations

The table began jumping about and rapping on the floor four times, meaning, it was explained, the sitters should talk. The curtains were thrown over the table, to the amusement of all. Immediately following this in quick succession came a number of manif estations, such as a hand appearing above the medium's head. Another hand was plainly seen placing the curtains over the table. A toy piano was thrown upon the table from over the medium's head. The table again was lifted and remained in the air about five seconds.

During this levitation I pressed with considerable force upon the table while it was suspended in the air.

Both controllers were touched several times on the head and arms by what they described as hands. The toy piano was raised in the air about four feet and thrown with great force upon the table, which startled us all.

The final effect was an ineffectual attempt to place a small chair upon the table, the chair having been previously placed in the cabinet.

The above manifestations were presented to us in such a way that we all agreed there was no explanation, for the control was maintained rigidly throughout, and if the controllers were not deceived by the medium, then it is fair to state that all those present accepted these effects as having been produced by an unknown force.

Trick Levitation Explained

In reviewing the above manifestations from a magician's standpoint it is necessary to explain the methods usually employed by mediums to produce similar effects by fraud.

The levitation of the table can be accomplished by one or more of the following methods:

1. A pin or small tack is driven into the table top, allowing the head only to project. This head is slipped into a slot in the medium's finger ring, and in that way the table is raised.

2. The medium might have concealed in her sleeves two pieces of wood extending through wristbands of leather. The wooden strips could be dropped down into the palm of the hand, the wood extending under the table top, and the hands resting on the top of the table, thus forming a sort of vise, by which pressure the table could be raised.

3. It is also possible for the medium to raise the table

by means of a thin wire attached around the neck, which would be hooked on to the table, and by the legs pressing against the medium's knees, and she throwing her head back, the table could be raised from the floor.

Apart from mechanical assistance, the most simple method would be the use of the hands, feet, and knees placed beneath the table top and beneath the legs nearest to her, and by a system of adroit leverage, the table could be completely raised from the floor for several seconds.

By accepting the statements of the controllers, I can definitely say these methods were not resorted to, because the hands could be plainly seen above the table, and at times not touching it, there being frequently a clear space between her body, as well as her feet and hands, and the table.

Not the Work of Medium

As to the cabinet phenomena, I cannot speak with equal certainty, owing to the reduction of the light, and being compelled to accept the statements of the controllers. I am certain, however, that the medium did not perform these effects with her own hands, for the light was sufficient to see them at all times. The 'spirit hands' were seen a foot above her head and to either side. It must be remembered her feet were tied to the chair, and at the end of the séance I personally cut the ropes that were binding her feet.

After the levitations, when the lights were being turned down, in preparing for the cabinet séance, they were completely extinguished for a few moments, apparently by mistake, and immediately after the lights were properly adjusted the curtains were thrown upon the table and a noise was heard in the cabinet. At this juncture, I, believing that someone had secretly entered the cabinet, asked to be permitted to examine it, but found no one concealed therein.

Suspicious Circumstances

Other occurrences which may be considered suspicious were, that most of the manifestations occurring on the séance table in front of us, such as placing the toy piano there and moving it about, were done while the curtains were partly covering the piano, thus making it possible for a person concealed behind the curtains to produce these effects, and several tines during these manifestations I believed there must have been someone concealed in the cabinet, for I could see plainly that the effects produced, such as touching the controller on the shoulder, lifting the piano, and producing visible hands at different parts of the curtain could not be performed by the medium, and if they were accomplished by trickery, it would have been necessary for someone to have been concealed in the cabinet.

With this feeling, I carefully watched for the exit of the secret assistant, and at the finish of the séance I quickly stepped to the curtains and examined them, but could find no evidence of anyone being there. Still, the lights were so dim that it could have been possible for an adroit and experienced person to have secretly entered and left the cabinet without being detected.

If I had been able to control the medium, personally, and these same manifestations had taken place, I would have felt convinced that there was an unknown force at work.

Could Not Detect Causes

The effect that has most forcibly been impressed upon my mind is the levitation of the table, which I had previously witnessed, and I must state that I could not discover the means employed.

The fact that we are accustomed to believe it is necessary to have physical contact with an object in order to move it is not positive proof that the object cannot be moved without physical contact, for we have in evidence such powers as are manifested in the magnet, by which objects can both be repelled and attracted without physical contact. The wireless telegraph will produce motion across the sea. The compass, the thermometer, and the barometer are all affected by unseen powers.

When we consider these mysterious forces which science has discovered, why should we not believe that it is possible for the human body to possess a power which we have not as yet discovered, and which would appear as mysterious as those until it had been explained?

from
THE NEW YORK TIMES

The Lady Journalist glided into Eusapia Paladino's dining room with a smile of tolerant awe on her face and a copy of last Sunday's paper in her hand. The pale-faced youth who accompanied her also wore a smile of awe, but there was no toleration in his glance, and in his hand he carried a suitcase containing his camera and flashlight apparatus.

Yes, La Paladino told Mme. La Giornalista, everything had been arranged for the séance at 10 o'clock. Meanwhile Mme. La Giornalista and her *Fidus Achates* were presented to the friends of La Paladino. These were Doctor Vecchio, an ancient friend and adviser extraordinary to the medium; Donato di Donato, the distinguished editor of a local italian paper; Signor Vigorito and Signora Vigorito, the latter well known in legal and real estate circles of Little Italy, and Signor Smeragiluolo, the artist, and his bride, Signora Smeragliuolo, who is the sister-in-law of La Paladino.

The presentations having been accomplished with all proper decorum, and the hour of 10 being nearly arrived, the company proceeded to the room where the table, the cabinet, the toy piano, and other implements of mediumistic craft had been arranged, and where John— John the arch-spirit, John the pirate—was supposed to be lurking in invisible yet potent fury.

Under the direction of the Lady Journalist, the palefaced youth with the camera set up his apparatus and opened his matchbox.

La Paladino seated herself, and, her new son-in-law having brought forth a bundle of quarter-inch hemp cord, they proceeded to tie her legs and her hands; then her wrists were attached to the right wrist of the Lady Journalist, who sat on her left, and to the left wrist of Signor di Donato, who sat at her right. Others at the table were Doctor Vecchio and the Vigoriti. The circle was formed. Either Signor Smeragliuolo or Signora Smeragliuolo— John did not observe which—turned the light very low.

"Controllo?" sternly inquired La Paladino. "Controllo?" repeated the Italians. "Controllo," echoed the Lady Journalist. Then everybody waited.

Except for the cries of the children in the street,

some voices in argument vociferating next door, and the rumble of an elevated train, all was quiet.

"Vieni, John!" commanded La Paladino. "Vieni, John," cried the Italians. "Come, John," whispered the Lady Journalist.

And John came.

Wonders for the Asking

As usual, the first evidence of his presence was manifested through the raising and swinging of the table. This so excited the youth with the photographic apparatus that he touched off a flashlight. The proceedings were interrupted until the windows could be opened and the room cleared of smoke.

The circle was restored and John set himself to work again. The object which first claimed his attention was the toy piano, then a chair. These he caused to hop about the roon and then, after a series of somersaults, to land on the table, where they remained long enough for the manipulator of the flashlight to take another picture.

There suddenly occurred a successive series of phenomena so sensational as profoundly to impress the sitters. A fluid hand which Doctor Vecchio recognized as that of his departed brother, after having tapped Signor di Donato on the chest a couple of times, drew from the latter's buttonhole a tearose which performed curious curves before the sitters and was finally fastened in the button hole of Doctor Vecchio's coat.

But this was not all. Suddenly the hand reappeared, this time bearing what seemed to be a human head, which, after it had made the round of the circle and had taken an aerial flight about the room, settled closely and caressingly against the face of Doctor Vecchio as though in the act of kissing him.

There were heard a number of loud blows, as from the strokes of a muscular hand, and this hand was felt in rude contact on the shoulders, the legs, the heads, and the faces of the sitters ; and then this hand became more aggressive and insinuating and finally brandished a stick, but the blows it delivered did harm to no one.

The curtain of the cabinet blew out like a sail, as though pressed forward by the cool, damp breeze that is wafted across graveyards, and, being thus pressed forward, it fell upon the table.

A weird shape now seemed to gather itself together in corporeal form, like the ghost of Hamlet's father on the ramparts ol Elsinore. The visitant hung low over Signor di Donato and articulated some meaningless words, such as Dante places in the mouth of Plutus: "Pape satan, pape satan, aleppe!"

The youthful illuminator of flashlights tipped over his camera, and suddenly sat down on his dress suitcase. The lady journalist fainted.

Dance of a Three-Legged Table

Fortunately, Doctor Vecchio was on hand, and John was kept waiting only a few moments. But John did not enjoy this waiting, and when the circle was restored he settled down to do his most artistic, diabolical work.

He first elevated the table three or four feet in the air ; he wrenched out one of the legs and brandished it before the sitters and pursued Smeragliuolo with it into a corner. Smeragliuolo was sore afraid. In the manner the stick was wielded he recognized the vanished hand of his departed mother.

Deprived of one of its legs the table became a prey to

furious dancing and weird, unholy noises, and shivering raspings as when an iron door long unused is shut and the rust falls from it. Sounds were heard emanating from the cabinet. Then the more gentle spirit which earlier in the séance had extracted the rose from Signor di Donato's buttonhole presented before him three carnations, one of which the spirit placed in his hand, and another in the hands of Doctor Vecchio, after tantalizing the Vigoriti with them.

Then came the end; the table turned a complete somersault and gave forth the seven ritualistic strokes of finality with so much force that its remaining legs were severed, while the toy piano swung in air, emitting notes of unknown melody from beyond the tomb.

Sundry Adjectives

There is, however, one point in the foregoing narrative which may not be confirmed by the story which the Lady Journalist is writing for her Sunday paper. While of no particular significance to either La Paladino or to John, it is of a certain importance to the Lady Journalist herself. It is this:

She declares that she did not faint. The fainting episode will, therefore, in all probability, not be found in her story. As to the rest, she was and is most enthusiastic. "Extraordinary! Marvelous! Wonderful!" were the words she used, and her *Fidus Achates* with the suitcase repeated them. As both expressed it later: In the humdrum commonplaceness of metropolitan Sunday feature gathering, they had at length experienced something new, felt a new sensation, a new emotion, utterly unlike anything they had encountered before.

As the Lady Journalist, the flashlight artist, and the

suitcase departed, the wreckage wrought by John was repaired and La Paladino and her Italian guests sat down to a cup of tea.

from
THE NEW YORK HERALD, DECEMBER 26, 1909

AN ACCOUNT
by
THE REVEREND FRANK LANDON HUMPHREYS, S.D.T.
(Late of the Cathedral of St. John the Divine)

I should like to say as a sort of preface that in writing Eusapia Paladino I have tried to write from the standpoint of an open, fair-minded observer, avoiding both the prejudice of the skeptical materialist and the credulity of the gullible spiritualist. Prepared to see something or nothing and with the intent to uncover fraud, if fraud existed, I have written of the phenomena as I saw them, and as a student of psychics and an explorer in a, to me, unknown country.

The theories and explanations of the foreign savants and of science concerning Eusapia are as hard for me to understand believe as the theories of the spiritualists. The theory a "fluidic arm" extended from her own person is as difficult for to accept as the theory of spirits, and does not explain how several things can be done at the same time, as is frequently the case. Those interested can read any amount of literature which has been published on the subject and decide for themselves.

At the same time the reading public might well be

cautioned against taking some newspaper reports too seriously. A daily paper that claims to be very careful about what it prints, failing to obtain a séance with Eusapia Paladino, promptly "faked" one, made up half of pure imagination and half of a rehash of facts apparently taken from a recently published book.

The little company that gathered in the corridor outside the door of the room in which we were to have a séance with this wonderful little Italian woman was quite heterogeneous in make-up. There were two stalwart young college professors of the Charles Dana Gibson type, vigorous of frame, clear-cut of feature, crisp and direct in conversation ; a gentleman representing the Society for Psychic Research, an old gentleman of very decidedly spiritualistic leaning ; his equally materialistic daughter, one other lady, and myself.

After waiting a few moments, the door was opened and we were invited to enter the room and examine its contents. The room was an ordinary room such as found in almost any office building, about twenty by fourteen feet. It had one small window on the side and two at the end facing the door. Between the small window in the side and the windows at the end there was built across the room a light, temporary partition of wood, which did not quite reach the ceiling ; at one end of it was a door leading back of the partition, through which one could enter and see that there was nothing on the other side.

The windows at this end were provided with a burglar alarm so that they could not be opened more than an inch without ringing a bell. There was nothing back of this partition except the windows and a radiator used for heating the room.

In the middle of this partition there was a built-in alcove about three feet deep and about eight feet high.

The American Séances

Across the front of this alcove were draped two black curtains of some very light and sheer material. Within the alcove there was a very small table and a stool, and some cheap musical instruments, such as an accordion, a music box, a tambourine, and also a bell.

We were invited to examine these instruments and note their position in the alcove, which served as a cabinet. We were also asked to examine this alcove and the partition and to look for wires or anything else which might suggest trickery or fraud.

After this examination was over, during which one of the young professors told me that they had spent two hours looking for anything in the way of small wires and cords or any other mechanical device, we came back into the front part of the room and met Eusapia Paladino, who meanwhile had come in with two Italian women and an interpreter.

Eusapia is a plain little Italian woman whose figure is decidedly below medium height, and suggests nothing of the spirit world. Her face, however, would arrest attention anywhere. It is a very strong face. Her eyes are keen and of tragic cast, and somehow continually reminded me of Edwin Booth. The spiritualistic gentleman whispered to me in awestruck tone, "She has the countenance of one directed by a higher power."

Eusapia was very direct and matter of fact in her conversation, and smiled very pleasantly once or twice while speaking to the ladies present. Soon divesting herself of her wraps, she seated herself directly in front of the black curtains, so that her chair was at a distance of about a foot from the curtains.

Then we were all invited to sit around the table which Eusapia drew before her. This table was a very ordinary light wooden affair, unpainted, built of white pine, apparently for use at the seance. Eusapia sat at the end of the table, and at her request on each side of her sat one of the young professors.

The rest of us gathered about the table and took our seats just as we happened to be standing. I sat at the end of the table, facing the medium. We were asked to join hands, each laying our hands very lightly on the table and linking our little fingers chain-fashion, except the two professors, who were to hold each of them one of Eusapia's hands.

In holding her hands they were requested not to press the backs of her hands, because they were extremely hyperesthetic during a séance, as were also the insteps of her feet. They also warned to keep track of the position of her feet by seeing that her right and left feet were placed upon the feet of the person seated next to her. They were also requested to feel any movement from her knee down to her feet by placing their knees against hers on each side, according to relative position.

The "circuit" having been made, we waited results. The room was still brilliantly lighted, there being no attempt to reduce light in any way. Eusapia glanced from one to another with quick, searching, tragic eyes, apparently to see if we were in sympathy with her, and I may say here that we were carefully warned not to openly show any attitude of skepticism or suspicion, as it would tend to prevent phenomena. Almost immediately Eusapia began to show evidences of being under great strain, by frequent sighings and by increased respiration, and one of the professors reported an increased pulse. Then the end of the table toward medium began to make short, jerky movements from side to side. After each movement there would be a few seconds' rest, then it would begin to move again, each time with increasing force.

Finally the end of the table near Eusapia began to lift from the floor, and as it lifted the young professors would report that were not touching the table other than to feel it rise under their hands. They also reported good "control," which meant they were holding Eusapia's hands and feet and that she could nowise lift the table herself. As the table began to rise from time to time a little higher, Eusapia showed signs of greater strain and greater exhaustion, until finally, after the table had risen completely, that isto say with both ends well elevated in the air, and remained there for a period of a second or two, it fell, as it always did after such risings, violently to its place on the floor.

Eusapia showed great exhaustion by her breath and groaning. Again and again the table rose in the air, each time a little higher, until finally, after, I should say, about twenty minutes twenty-five minutes of effort, the table rose in the air at least a foot and remained there without any visible means of support two or three seconds, when it again fell violently to its place on the floor.

The medium, recovering from her momentary exhaustion, suggested that I change places with the professor on her left, which was immediately done. She grasped my hand firmly and placed her left foot as firmly across mine. I could feel the movements of her leg to the knee, and several times during the subsequent levitations of the table she took my hand and placed it on her knee to show that there was absolutely no muscular effort as the table was again lifted several times from the floor and remained suspended in the air for a second or two. During these phenomena we were not only allowed, but urged to talk among ourselves, being informed that it assisted in the production of phenomena.

Finally the lights were turned down, still allowing one red electric bulb, which was enough to see dimly the faces and figures of those about us. We were warned 'not to break the chain,' but to place ourselves in sympathy with the medium and wait.

Before long the left curtain began to reach out, as if blown by some silent breeze. It would blow out so as to touch the medium and those about her and then drop back. Sometimes it extended far enough to cover her hand and that of one of the professors. Then one of the sitters reported that he had been touched on the shoulder, though it was quite apparent that no one was near him. Others reported from time to time that they were touched, and in one instance one said he was grasped by an invisible hand. Then, while the curtain was blown out well toward the end of the table, there came from it, and from over the left shoulder of Eusapia, what seemed to be a long black arm with a shapeless hand almost the size of a boxing glove. This appeared six times and disappeared. Then a small table or stool was thrown violently from behind the curtains.

Some one was requested to go quickly behind the curtains and see if any one was there. The gentleman from the Society for Psychic Research very quickly stepped behind the curtains and reported that there was no one behind them and that everything seemed to be in its proper place except the small table, which had been thrown out into the room.

As he came out from behind the curtains into the room he reported that his hand had been grasped as by another hand. Resuming our places at the table, after a moment a white arm came forth again from over the medium's left shoulder, if it could be called an arm, for it hardly had that appearance in the gloom, nor did it seem to end in a hand, but in an oval object about the size of a child's head, and it seemed to be luminous.

Toward the close of the séance Eusapia would take the hands of those seated next to her and hold them against the curtain where it bulged out, and they would report a solid, material, unyielding pressure. A gentleman seated near me said that at another séance at which be had been present one could feel the pressure of a hand or the form of a face. I am sorry that I, having changed my seat, so that I no longer sat near Eusapia, could not feel any of these phenomena. What I saw, however, was enough to be most astonishing, and I must confess to feeling quite uncanny as the phenomena and noises behind the curtains increased, as if things were being moved about in a very lively fashion.

As the seance progressed, Eusapia seemed to go into a kind of trance—constantly groaning and sighing and hiccoughing. At last she seemed to collapse utterly, and with a general crash from everything behind the curtains falling to the floor the séance was declared over. She seemed to be some time coming to herself, and the Italian women gathered about her and gave her water and did what they could to make her comfortable.

The lights being fully turned up, some of us walked behind the curtains into the recess, or cabinet. The place looked as though it had been struck by a cyclone. Everything wa in confusion, strewn all about the floor. This was exhibited by the psychic side of our little party with considerable pride, though I confess that it did not appeal to me after the astonishing things I had just seen. At the end of the séance I talked with one of the young professors, who did not seem to care to commit himself as to any possible explanation of the phenomena we had just witnessed. At the sarnc time we could not doubt that these things were beyond explanation under ordinary physical laws as we have been taught to understand them. We neither of us felt that spirits had anything to do with the phenomena, and were both disappointed that so much of the séance had been spoiled by the constant interruptions of the spiritualist calling for spirits to manifest themselves and for table knockings and the like.

At the second séance, we had a much more congenial party and the results plainly showed in the increased phenomena. There were no women and the gathering around the table was made up of men whose names are well known. On my right and next to Eusapia was an admiral who has served his country with distinction.

As at the previous séance, we began with levitations of the table. The table began to move almost at once and, not to dwell upon this matter, already made familiar, I can only say that finally we all moved our chairs well back from the table, taking our hands from it entirely and making a circle as large as our extended arms would allow, and the table arose from the floor about fourteen inches and remained in the air with no one touching or near it for four seconds before falling back to the floor.

Eusapia then curled her feet up under her on the chair, to show that her feet were not near the table, and making the circle still wider the same thing occurred. This was the most convincing proof that no trickery could be possibly used.

Then, taking our seats, the curtain began to blow out, as at the previous séance. Presently a tambourine rolled out from behind the curtains and other sounds seemed to show activity there. I noticed something on Eusapia's head, as I thought, but before I could see what it was a small music box half fell and half floated to the table, for that was what it turned out to be. I say half floated, for it came so slowly and softly as to seem to have lost the property of weight. 1 at once picked it up, for it landed exactly in front of me.

Then came from behind the table the sound of creaking wood and straining cords, and we were informed by one of the party that he had tied the table to the floor by cords running through screw eyes screwed into the floor. This sound continued from time to time throughout the seance. But the power used was not sufficient to break either the table or the cords, though we found the cords stretched considerably at the end of the séance.

Now, from time to time different ones around the table would declare that they had been touched or grasped. Then one by one all left the table by turn, and felt the curtains as they blew out, and the astonishment of some was very evident as they reported feeling active resistance to pressure on the curtain or the grasp of a hand, as the case might he. I confess that I felt some reluctance when my turn came. Placing my hand as high upon the curtain as possible, say seven feet, I felt most distinctly the gentle touch of four fingertips upon the palm of my hand. It was a most human touch, and I almost pinched myself to ascertain if I was awake. Of course, you will understand that we constantly looked behind the curtain, and that at times it puffed out so far that those sitting near could see behind it.

Then there appeared over Eusapia's head a small hand and part of an arm. It was not at all like the rather shapeless appearance at the previous séance, but beautifully formed and apparently flesh colored, but as these things flash out only for a second or a fraction of a second, one has to watch constantly not to lose anything, and often only some of the party would see and report an appearance.

About this time, with a noise as if being dragged, a small stool came out from under the curtain and tried to climb on the table between the admiral and Eusapia. The admiral placed his hand upon its top, reported quite a pressure, as the stool would try to rise high enough to get up on top of the table. It was really amusing to watch this little green stool wabble out into view and try over and over again to climb up, only to fall back. Several times it was picked up and examined for cords or anything of the kind, and as soon as put down began again its efforts. I am sorry to say that it did not succeed, and we finally shoved it over in a corner, where it remained the rest of the evening.

The admiral now reported that a greenish or bluish light had appeared at the opening of the curtain near his head, and a gentleman at the other end of the table said that a cheek had been caressingly placed against his. A great noise came from behind the curtains. Eusapia said she was dying, and the seance was declared at an end.

Eusapia showed more complete exhaustion than at the previous séance, and was quite sick, and while her relatives were taking care of her most of us left, being unable to do anything to assist in the care of this marvellous little woman.

The third séance was the most astonishing and bears out the claim that Eusapia's powers increase as the sittings are continued. The personnel of our party was only slightly changed by the addition of a stout man, who was quite sceptical and said that he had been for forty years looking for phenomena and finding only fraud. This was promptly interpreted to Eusapia, who immediately chose him for control on her left side, holding her left hand

and foot.

The séance began with the usual levitations of the table, which I pass over as already sufficiently described, only pausing to note the half-incredulous astonishment of the stout skeptic. The phenomena following were slower in coming than usual, and Eusapia complained that our stout friend was "hard." When they came, however, they first frightened him to no small degree and then converted him. The lights were not turned down quite as low as usual, allowing a very fair light to see with, and after the curtains had begun to puff out in the usual fashion, phenomena followed each other with remarkable rapidity. First the tambourine came out over Eusapia's head and fell lightly upon the table. Then a black arm came out and tapped our skeptical friend lightly on the head and shoulder.

We then all united in asking that an impression be made in some wet clay which I had prepared and placed in three boxes behind the curtains. We could hear the usual sounds and movements behind the curtains, but could only guess at what was going on. Presently one of the boxes of clay was brought and dropped before me. It was quite heavy, but made little noise as it fell in front of me, as if it fell only an inch or two, if that much, or seemed rather to be placed roughly on the table. It bore no mark or impression on its surface.

The skeptical stout man reported repeatedly in an excited tone that he had been touched or grasped, as the case might be, but that he still held Eusapia's hand and foot. Intent as I was in watching, I could not but be amused at his mixture of delighted discovery and more than half-frightened wonder and astonishment. Then a chair was brought out and placed before him on the table.

We asked that the mandolin be played behind the curtains. In a few seconds we began to hear it move, the strings occasionally sounding as it appeared to be slowly rolling about. Finally it seemed to get into a position where by turning from side to side it could rub the strings against some object and so make them sound. This continued for a minute or more. Then Eusapia called for the lights to be turned down lower, and only one red incandescent globe was left. Presently in the gloom we could see moving lights of a greenish phosphorescent kind, like gigantic fireflies, all about Eusapia, and in some cases flying off and disappearing in the distance.

The mandolin then suddenly made its appearance over the skeptic's head, playing as it came. He cried out that it had struck him lightly three times on the head, but that he still held Eusapia. He held his hands up either to protect himself or to catch hold of the mandolin. It immediately came over to our side of the table, quite visible, in the air above our heads, and still playing, until it finally was placed on the table before me, where I could see it plainly, even in the diminished light, and hear the strings sound, though I could not see them vibrate.

This was one of the most convincing as well as most astonishing of the various phenomena I observed—the mandolin, lying directly in front of me, and so plainly visible, making a sound as if some hand swept its strings, while I could see nothing but the instrument itself.

A number of other phenomena occurred, such as I have already described, and at the end of the séance there was the usual tumult behind the curtains and the usual effort to bring Eusapia out of the trancelike state into which she seems to fall, and out of which she comes with such complete exhaustion.

Going behind the curtains I found my other two boxes of wet clay thrown on the floor. I observed with disappointment, as I picked them up, that only one had any kind of an impression on it, and that only a slight one. I had hoped to find the impression of a face such as the foreign savants secured. The one that was marked had the impression of the backs of three fingers, showing the fingers from the middle joints to the nails. The nails were very plainly discernible.

The curious thing which I noted was that the clay was so wet that when anyone touched it some of it always came away on the fingers, leaving a rough impression. The impression I found was very smooth.

This I had purposely arranged, for I have had considerable experience in using clay in modelling and I wanted to detect anybody tampering with the boxes. Clay dries quickly on the hands, leaving a white line around the nails which it is quite difficult to wash off and cannot possibly be quickly wiped off. I could not find, and hardly expected to find, any evidence of clay on Eusapia's hands, since she was held so well by the control.

From what I saw, I can only come to the conclusion that this abnormal woman has some peculiar power through an unknown physical force—a power that we all ought to have and may yet develop in the future. I believe that this power is shown in such parlor tricks as the lifting of one person on the single finger tips of a few others, and a number of other similar performances.

These facts are none the less wonderful because they are purely material. On the contrary, I think that the interest is increased because of this extension of half-known or the application of entirely unknown physical forces and laws. And I look forward toward the future, when all this will not only be thoroughly understood, but when these forces will he controlled and used by everyone.

Printed in Great Britain
by Amazon